About the Book

*Foot*ball is the name of the game, and although carrying the ball over the goal line is what piles up most of the points, the game cannot be won—or even played—without the kickers. Here, for the athlete who yearns for a place on the team, are the secrets of the place-kick, the punt, the running kick, the quick kick, and the dropkick.

Dedication

This book is dedicated to my wife of forty seven years who has tolerated my absences from home and the many telephone calls which interrupted family living while developing the information in this book.

Also, to all the boys who have been my students and because of my encouragement have put in hours and hours of practice to attain their skill. Their successes provide my thrills.

How to Kick the

FOOTBALL

Edward J. "Doc" Storey

Leisure Press

West Point, N.Y. • Berkeley, CA

Library of Congress Catalog Card Number: LC 80-83979
ISBN 918438-61-6

Text illustrations by Elizabeth Williams.

Front and back cover photographs of Michael Rendina, Jr. The photograph on
page 125 is by John Copeland, courtesy of the *Miami Herald*.

Acknowledgements

The author has received much information from interested people during the development of the material that is in this book and he wishes to give them credit for their contribution. Among these people are, Dr. Frank Downing, Dr. Richard Gerson, Michael Rendina, Joe Campenella, Dr. R.M. Salvino, J.M. Mather, Fred O'Keefe and Mike Farley, with whom he has been associated for six years as an instructor in his kicking camps.

There are always new ideas and thoughts concerning the development of a skill. The author has received ideas and stimulation from the reading of two special books - **The Inner Athlete** by Robert M. Nideffer and **The Inner Game of Tennis** by W. Timothy Gallwey. Another very valuable book for me was **Patterns of Human Motion** by Stanley Plagenhoef of the University of Massachusetts.

If the author had never met Leroy N. Mills in 1928, this book could have never happened. He took me as a neophyte in the late twenties and taught me what he knew about kicking the football. It gave me the desire to know more about the science of propelling the prolate spheroid. Wherever he may be, I am sure that he will be pleased to see this material in print. His ideas pervade my teaching.

The author also wants to thank all sports writers, who by their incisive questioning have made the author think more intensely about his theories and scientific explantations. Prominent among these has been William N. Wallace of the *New York Times*.

Edw. J. Storey

Contents

Forwards

FORWARD

Doc Storey came into my life in the lobby of a Miami Beach hotel a few days before a Super Bowl game - I have forgotten which one but perhaps the second one in the Orange Bowl, which would make it January, 1969, the match between the Baltimore Colts and the New York Jets which a few of us remember.

Doc and I talked in the lobby for at least an hour (I remember the talk better than the game, obviously). It was soon apparent to me that Doc Storey not only knew what he was talking about but that he had few listeners. I became one, and have been ever since. The purpose of this book is to make more.

Although Doc has me by a few decades as to age, our talk on that morning in a garish hotel lobby came easily and I had enough football history in me, forinstance, to know about Leroy Mills when that name came up. Mills was the first man to be totally appreciative about the possibilities of the foot in football, meaning the kicking game. He was a man of small stature like Doc, wore knickers and smoked a pipe. So equipped, at a ripe old age he continued to kick the hell out of the football. A Princeton man, Mills longed for the day when the coaches would call him back to Nassau Hall to teach the tactics and strategy of the foot in football. After almsot half a century the story is clouded so we do not know whether they ever did, or if Mills died, never having the chance to prove his point.

Storey admired Mills much as E.B. White, that impeccable essayist, admired Professor Strunk, White's mentor in the use of the English language at Cornell. No Strunk, no White. No Mills, no Storey.

White's exquisite language lives on and so does Doc Storey's postulation about the foot in football. The analogy is so far fetched, because Storey brings so many other elements to kicking the football. The kick in the game of football evokes elements of physiology, of physics, of boldness, of risk, of training and discipline - and I hope some humour. Doc Storey, above all else, is equipped with what I like to call H. & H., humour and humility.

The author of this book credits me with having been his first booster because of my occasional articles about him in the publications for which I am lucky enough to write, the *New York Times* and *Pro Football Weekly*.

If he is correct, I am pleased because then I have accomplished something - I have helped call attention to a man who knows what he is talking about, as the reader is about to discover.

Knowledge comes in many forms about many subjects. There can be no value judgement as to what kind of knowledge is more important than any other. The sum of all knowledge is our nation, our culture, our ambitions, our disappointments. To be thoroughly knowledgable about any subject, whether it be stamps, the banjo, atomic energy, the birch-bark canoe, is all of a part.

To know and teach the myriad ways to kick a football so as to effect the outcome of a game, any game from Mamaroneck High against White Plains to a match of Super Bowl opponents, is a part of the whole, an accomplishment of merit.

William N. Wallace
New York Times

FORWARD

When I first met Doc Storey, he was sitting in his study at his Fort Lauderdale home, looking at a football. "I believe I've seen just about everything that can happen when a foot strikes a football," he said. And as our friendship grew through the next few weeks and months, I came to believe him.

Doc regaled me with wild stories of punted balls travelling a hundred yards (or minus twenty yards), of field goal attempts that came to rest on goal posts, of 50-year-old men punting forty-yarders that spun out of bounds on the one-foot line. The story I was writing for **Sports Illustrated** grew and grew until I had to tell Doc to stop, to hold the facts before I ended up writing a multi-volume epic.

The point is: Doc **has** seen it all. A few years ago the **N.Y. Times** called him "the greatest living authority on punting." As player, coach, camp director, school administrator, fan, he's made the study of booting "the prolate spheroid" his hobby, his obsession, his **raison d'etre.** Doc's enthusiasm spans the modern game: he was friends with Knute Rockne; he organized his first kicking camp in 1932; he helped Woody Umphrey punt Alabama to victory in the 1978 and 1979 Sugar Bowls.

At 79 Doc is spry and outspoken as ever, and he still knows his stuff. While this book may not turn you into a Ray Guy or a Lou "The Toe" Groza overnight, as anybody in the kicking business can tell you, it's a darn good place to start.

Rick Telander
Sports Illustrated

Introduction

The name of the game is *football*. Even today, the day of the wide-open game with flankers, setbacks, long passes, the pro T formation, and split ends, the kick remains a fundamental and vital element in the game when you are playing to win. Not too many players or coaches, however, seem to realize this truth, and so you can have an advantage. Learn to kick the football where you want to kick it, and you will have a distinct advantage over other players and other teams.

You don't have to be the best athlete around school in order to be the best kicker. You must educate your balance before you educate your toe. And you'd better learn *how* to kick before experience teaches you *when* to kick. Maybe you don't want to be the just "toe" brought in from the bench to try the "point after." You want to play the game. That's what we want you to do. We want you to be an expert at football.

You can use your foot and play a scoring game, a defensive game, surely a clutch game, even an offensive game to get good position for your team on the field. In this book we'll consider the place kick, the punt, the running kick, quick kick, and the drop kick.

You haven't heard about the drop kick and the running kick? Your friends will get a great surprise when you show them how they are done.

When not otherwise specified, we will be considering the art of kicking from the standpoint of the right-footed kicker. The left-footed kicker merely reverses the lefts and rights. A little later on, we'll see how these kicks fit into the overall strategy of the game. Now let's get started.

THE GAME OF FOOTBALL

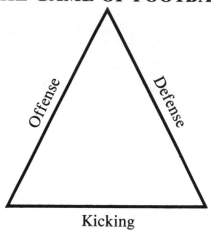

THE KICKING GAME OF FOOTBALL

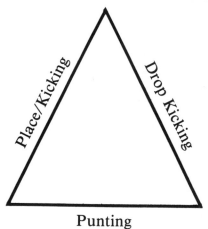

1
The Key Is Balance

Because kicking the football is one of the few skills that an athlete must perform on one foot, balance is the first consideration. It isn't speed, strength, or judgment that is the important element of kicking. Balance is!

Later we'll get into the other elements of kicking: aiming, placing the ball on your foot, timing, and follow-through. But before you can be an accurate kicker, you must have excellent balance as a firm foundation from which to kick. What is good balance, and how can you achieve it?

When man developed from being a four-footed animal millions of years ago and stood on two feet, he had great difficulty. All you have to do to understand this difficulty is watch a baby try to take his first steps. It may take him almost two years to become proficient at walking on two feet. Have you ever been confined to bed for a few weeks? If so, remember that you had to start walking very slowly when you first got up.

Standing up or standing up straight is one of the most difficult problems that human beings have. It has been said that walking a tight rope can be done much more easily by grownups than for babies to learn to just stand up and walk. No one stands still for a minute. The instinctive urge is to move. Watch any group of people standing around and see how quickly they move one way or another. The reason is that walking or moving is much easier on the body's muscles than standing like a soldier at attention.

Man has evolved from four-footed locomotion to two-footed locomotion, and ability to balance on one foot.

The fundamental difficulty in standing up straight is that the human body was never designed for standing on two legs. It was designed to be used on all fours like a dog or a cat. Our organs hang from the spinal column like clothes hanging from a line. The spine was designed to be horizontal, not vertical as we use it. It is a girder by design, not a column.

When a human being is standing up straight on two feet, he is using about three hundred muscles in the body to achieve this position and to hold it. To move takes about one half that number of muscles. The failure of any of the muscles holding the body erect means a collapse of the whole body.

Researchers tell us that we each have a "superintendent of balance" in the lower part of the brain - a sort of central computer for balance. Information to this center comes from four sources. First there are the eyes which record any imbalance as the body tips. Then there are the ears. The semi-circular canals of the ear act as controls for balance in the body. These are like carpenter's levels which record the position of the head and tell the posture center in the lower brain exactly which direction in space the head is going.

A third source of information comes from the two small cavities located in the head bones just behind the ears. These two small cavities contain tiny grains of mineral matter resting in a network of fine living fibers. When one's head is laid on its side or on its back, these mineral grains press in different directions on the fibers. This sends a message to the brain center notifying it that the head is bent over in one direction or the other.

Fourth, and perhaps more important than the semi-circular canals, the mineral grains and the eyes, is the mechanism which originates in the muscles themselves. From every muscle, every joint, every bone, there are nerves which take information to the balance center. Much of this information is not carried to the thinking part of the brain. However, these sensations and the information carried is most important to the reflexes including those which keep the body standing. It is all of these that operate the posture center.

Every instant a person stands erect, thousands of nerve messages are going into the posture center in the lower brain and thousands of others are coming out from it to the several hundred muscles which bring the body back when it starts to topple. The reason for fatigue when standing is that these "pulls" need to be so much more continuous and rapid than when the body is moving, just as a bicyclist needs to be more alert to balance himself when he is standing still.

Probably the busiest place in a person's body when he is standing still is the tiny nerve center in his lower brain. This is what we have to be aware of when considering balance - especially when we have to stand on one foot for about one hundredth of a second while kicking the football.

Now it should come as no shock for you to discover that there are problems in mastering the art of standing on one foot and stroking the football with the other foot, which is what you do when you kick a football.

Try standing on your left foot (right foot for left-footed kickers). How long can you do it before you must put your other foot down to regain your balance? Try it again. You must stand on that foot under control while your kicking leg swings under the football, propels it forward, and then comes back to the ground in the same position or stance. Of course, you cannot do the whole sequence effectively now. But by using certain exercises, you will improve your balance.

Stand on your balance foot again, and then pedal with your kicking foot as though you had a bicycle that you were pedaling with one leg. How many times can you do it before you have to catch yourself? Thirty times? Forty? When you can do it 100 times, you are getting started. I have had some young kickers who could do it 300 times and then ask me if they could stop. Practice this exercise, and your balance will get to be what you want for kicking.

Body balance depends on the semicircular canals in your ears. If you are suffering from a very high fever or cold, your balance will probably be affected. Also, any accident to your head can affect these canals and thereby affect your balance and your kicking.

Let's try again to stand on that balance foot (left for right-footed kickers) without using your kicking foot as we give some more consideration to your balance. Get your shoemaker to put a long bar cleat lengthwise on the heel of the shoe of your balance foot. It will help anchor this foot to the ground in whatever direction you want to kick. This balance foot is also referred to as the anchor and directional foot.

When people walk or move, they tend to walk with their feet parallel. If your left foot is pointed straight ahead and you lift your right leg to move ahead, it will naturally move in the direction of the left foot. This is why the placement of your left foot determines largely the direction of the football when it is kicked.

Take a step and try putting your left foot down firmly on the ground with all the cleats in contact. Now swing your right leg and see if you can keep the left foot in place. The idea is to produce a rigid column with your hip locked above your left foot and your head sitting on top. This rigid column supports the power of your right leg in motion.

You place considerable stress on your body in the act of kicking, and you cannot support this stress with footholds of air or while standing on tiptoe or even on the ball of your foot. You need solid footing in order to control the kicking effort and to get all possible power into the propulsion of the football.

Physical activity, though, is not all you need for developing perfect balance. Your mind also plays a big role. Every day as you walk, say to yourself, "Balance foot, kicking foot, left foot, right foot. . ." and so on. Such activity helps set nerve switches and starts a new habit of thinking about kicking. If you are a left-footer, you of course call your right foot your balance foot. It's even possible that you may be a switch kicker. In the history of football there have been some famous men who could kick with either foot.

The kicking stance. Inset shows how kicking foot should be four inches ahead of the balance foot.

Getting Set — Your Ready Position

Every sport has one or more "get set" positions. You are probably familiar with some of them in tennis and golf. The "get set" position is also a must in kicking the football. You need to have a position that will guarantee that you can unleash all possible power under the football when you wish to apply it. The correct position will make the ball go where you want it to go. This position is commonly called your kicking stance.

Any mistakes that you make at the beginning of your kick may produce serious consequences. You want to have a stance that will accomplish the quickest possible completion of the entire kicking movement. Such a stance is fundamental to all kicking.

Your objective should be to develop a stance that will allow you to kick with just one step, or perhaps a step and a half. You'll practice this stance until it becomes almost automatic.

Stand with your kicking foot about 4 inches in front of your balance foot with your balance foot toes even with the base of your kicking foot toes. Your feet should be about as far apart as the distance across your hips (roughly 8-10 inches). Check to see that from the knees down your legs are parallel and the same distance apart.

The reason for having the kicking foot ahead is to provide a kind of brace to prevent you from falling back when the ball is snapped from center. Also, all humans have a tendency to fall backward rather than forward under any upsetting conditions. Man's spinal column was designed for four-footed walking, and the curves it has seem to balance us backward. With your kicking foot ahead and your weight on both feet, you have your best balance to move and kick forward.

As soon as you think you have found a comfortable stance, get a large piece of paper, stand on it, and with a crayon draw on it an outline of your feet in your "get set" position. This simple illlustration will help you get yourself into the habit of standing this way. Step off the paper and see if you can jump back onto it in the same position.

Out on the practice field try jumping into this stance. Practice jumping with your feet in this position around to the east, then to the north, and then to the south. Are your feet in the same relative position? Is your kicking foot 4 inches in front of your balance foot? Are your feet the right distance apart? This is one exercise you should do every day. Before you kick a ball, this is the "get set" position that you'll always take.

Someday, when you are in punting a game and the center gives you a bad pass, you must remember to go get the ball and not reach for it. After you get the ball, you jump into your "get set" position and then kick it. When you have a defensive line rushing in on you, there'll be no time to think about getting into position. This action must be automatic. Until you have achieved this feeling of being comfortable in this stance, don't try kicking.

If the center passes you a ball that rolls on the ground, practice fielding it as you would if you were a shortstop. Then pivot and, if you are right footed, spin counter clockwise, take a couple of steps, and kick it as you usually do. This pivot play is especially successful because the pivot places you behind the defensive men who have attempted to block the kick. They will no longer interfere with your kick. The momentum created by this stunt will give you a fine punt.

Another fine exercise to help you to get comfortable in your stance is to start running, stop quickly, jump into a stance, then turn around and run in a different direction. Do the same thing again. Practice this maneuver every day.

There is a lot of thinking needed if you are to be a great kicker. For instance, every night just before you turn over to go to sleep, you might think about your stance. Imagine that you are looking at your feet in this stance. Be sure your kicking foot is 4 inches ahead of the balance foot. Are your feet the right distance apart? Keep thinking about this stance until you go to sleep. This mental activity will help make getting into your stance as automatic as you want it to be. Then you can think about the kicking motion.

To Make It Go Where You Want It to Go

The only way to be certain that the football will go where you want it to go is to aim it. Your left foot is your aiming foot if you are a right-footed kicker. When your left foot is aimed at your target and stays firmly on the ground while you kick the ball, the football will go there just as surely as if you had a computer aiming it. This aiming foot, a very important part of kicking, is also the balance-anchor foot. Keep that left foot on the ground and you will avoid many errors that other kickers make.

When a kicker makes the mistake of leaving the ground, his fundamental instincts make him get back to it as soon as possible. When his body is in the air, it is out of control. So is his kick. He falters in the propelling of the ball, and he never gets his whole power into the kick. Often you see a kicker whose foot seems to punch the ball and who leaves the ground during the kick. This flaw prevents a smooth follow-through.

Any kicker who leaves the ground wastes a great deal of energy. If you multiply the number of pounds of the kicker by the distance he rises from the ground, you will have the number of foot-pounds of energy he has used.

19

The kicking foot lifts the ball off the ground, but the balance foot remains on the ground.

This energy cannot be used to lift the football if the kicker uses it to lift himself off the ground. But the most damaging effect of leaving the ground is the loss of accuracy.

When you aim the kick by aiming your left foot, you want the ball to go in that direction. That's exactly what happens if you stay on the ground.

When a right footed kicker leaves the ground, he pulls his kick to the left. This happens because the driving power comes from the right side of his body and because most kickers cross their leg over to the inside. There is a turning effect on the body when there is no anchoring of the balance foot. The left foot of the right footed kicker loses its aiming effect and the kick may go anywhere, usually it is a slice.

It is normal for a kicker to cross his leg over in the follow through unless some special training has taken place because the adductor muscles of the leg are normally stronger than the abductors (which pull the leg away from the mid-line of the body). To develop the strength in abductors which will prevent the cross-over, lie on your left side and swing the right leg up and down as many times as possible each day. This simple exercise, repeated a couple of hundred times each day, will make possible a straight swing of the leg all the way through.

The development of a good swing up of the left arm for a right footed kicker is most important. It is the helper arm. Human beings are bilateral. This means that, when we run, the arm swings the opposite leg. This is true in getting the best swing of the leg when kicking the football. When you see a kicker with a lazy arm, you can be sure that he is not getting all the impact on the ball that he could have.

The record shows that most field goals missed by right-footed kickers are missed to the left of the goalposts. In the Super Bowl of 1969, Lou Michaels of the Baltimore Colts, a *left-footed kicker,* missed all his crucial kicks to the right of the goalposts. This is the tendency of left-footed kickers. If those kicks had been made, Baltimore would have been the world's champions. All that was needed was for him to aim to the left upright.

2
How to Punt the Football

Now that you have begun to get familiar with the problems of balance and getting set, you can start to get into the actual kicking. In a typical game, you'll punt more than you'll do any other kind of kicking, so you probably want to begin mastering this kick first.

The punting of a football, the prolate spheroid, depends largely upon two factors — the momentum of the kicker and the collision of the ball and his foot. This foot and ball collision is known as an elastic collision in physics because the football returns to its original shape after the collision. How far the punt goes depends to a great extent on the speed of the foot at contact. The ball leaves the punter's foot at twice the speed of the foot.

For the greatest distance, the ball must leave the foot at a 45 degree angle to the ground. The resultant trajectory is a parabola, not a semi-circle. Therefore, at times there is no advantage to a very high kick because distance on the ground can be lost.

The momentum transfer is important. We believe in having the punter take what amounts to a step and a half before making the kick because the first step is short in order to get the body into motion quickly and efficiently. The object is to get the fastest possible speed of the body and then quickly transfer it to the leg, foot and the ball. All practices should keep this in mind - practice speed, speed and more speed.

There are basically two kinds of punts:

- The spiral (right and left).
- The end-over-end punt.

When you achieve punting skill, you'll be able to kick the ball where you want and with the type of kick you decide to use. Your coach may want the kick high or low, and you must be able to act accordingly.

Now you should start to practice the right way of holding the ball and placing it on your foot. These skills are necessary in getting the maximum propulsion of the ball toward your chosen spot. To be a consistent kicker, you must lay the ball on your foot the same way every time for the same kick. A crucial element is how you hold the ball. You must do it in such a way that you can lay it on your foot easily and accurately. After you have learned to handle the ball with sureness, you'll have no fear of juggling it at a critical moment.

Holding a football the right way for kicking is about like holding a platter of food. You simply place the middle finger of your right hand under the ball on the middle seam. The laces are on top. Every time you get a ball in your hands, immediately place that middle finger under the ball on the middle seam. Eventually you'll be able to do it with your eyes closed. The more you spread your fingers, the better grip you'll have on the ball.

Now place your left hand on top of the ball near the front and in any spot that you wish. This left hand (for a right-handed kicker) is a balance hand and is not essential in holding the football. It is the first one you remove from the ball (because of our bi-lateralism this is the helper arm that should swing upward with the swing of the right leg).

Your right hand when it is under the football tends to point to the left. When you take your right hand away and allow the ball to lie on your ankle, the long axis of the ball will lie generally diagonally across your ankle. The resulting kick will be a spiral. This spiral is called a left spiral because the front point of the ball points to the left. Sometime when you have your shoes and socks off, take a felt marker and draw a line on your foot. Start the line at the base of your big toe and run it to the midpoint of the outside line of your foot. This is the line the football must be on with the long axis in order to give you the ideal position for the left spiral.

Even some places indoors you can lay the ball on this line and pass it with your foot without kicking. This line on your foot is called the first metatarsal line. It connects the first metatarsal bone with the midline of the outside of your foot. If the football is kicked with the seam in front of this line on the foot, you lose power. If the seam is in back of this line, you'll not have a smooth spiral. If you are left-footed, then of course you'll do the foregoing with your left foot.

Kicking the football is the result of a collision of the foot and the ball. Ideally, we want this collision to take place with the ball in position on the foot so that its center of gravity and the center of gravity of the foot is in the same vertical line. An anatomy book will show this to be where the navicular bone and cuneiform bones come together, the most rigid part of the foot. Then we will have the most efficient transfer of momentum from the body to the leg, foot and the ball. It may be interesting to note that the ball being propelled weighs only 15 ounces and does not require extremely strong legs to propel it. What it does require is a fast foot because the ball leaves the foot at twice the speed of the foot. Exercising to become a good kicker must include activities which have to be practiced at speeds. Sprints, plyometrics, and other exercises of that type are recommended.

By holding the ball with your middle finger under the middle seam, you're always in control of the ball, and you can change the position of the football on your foot at the last instant before kicking it. By elevating your middle finger, you can make the football go high, and by depressing the finger, you can keep the football's trajectory low. By moving the base of the middle finger to the right, you can make the ball's middle seam correspond with the midline of your foot and thereby produce an end-over-end punt.

Now you should try one more drill before the actual kicking: Practice *passing* the ball with your kicking foot.

You start this maneuver by standing on your balance foot and placing the ball on your foot with the midseam on that metatarsal line and with only one finger on top of the laces. Now lift your foot and try to pass the ball to someone. When your foot comes up, depress your toe and the ball will roll off into a left spiral.

After you have done this often enough to start getting the idea of passing left spirals with your foot, try putting the ball on your ankle with the midseam pointed straight ahead. The belly of the ball will fit easily into the curve of your ankle. Pass this ball with a finger on top to balance it and you have the end-over-end punt. You ought to practice this exercise every day at least fifty times. And it's a good way to discover what you are doing wrong whenever kicks are not going well in the future. This is an exercise always to come back to. Be certain during this exercise that your balance-anchor foot is firmly on the ground.

How the ball is held. Inset shows location of first metatarsal line.

As you continue to practice this skill, try to keep your ankle under the ball longer and longer. Also, practice depressing your toe more and more. You should release the ball before your leg has risen to a position straight out from your hip. After that, your toe will come back on the ball and make it go high; you won't be able to control it.

Check your heel and toe cleats of your kicking shoe. They should be shorter than the other cleats on your shoe. On the heel of the balance foot, I like to have a long cleat lengthwise of the heel. Such a cleat helps direct this foot and hold it firmly.

Even such a seemingly small detail as how you tie your shoelaces is important in kicking. There should be no knot in front. The knot should be tied in back or at the side. You can even use a piece of adhesive tape across the laces to make sure there is nothing on your ankle to hinder good contact with the football. If you see a kicker who has his shoelaces tied behind, it's a good bet that he has been taught some fundamentals of kicking.

A high shoe is preferable to a low cut one but it is hard to find. A leather shoe is preferable to canvas shoes. Ideally for kicking the shoe should have a steel shank for each arch support that does not flex. Otherwise it is like parking a heavy weight on a plank spanning a ditch; the plank may sink at midpoint. So may the unprotected longitudinal arch. As we have noted previously, leather is preferable because it is porous. It lets the foot breathe and get rid of accumulating moisture. When buying new kicking shoes, put them on, get them soaking wet, then wear them on the field and let them dry slowly. They will assume the shape of your foot and will be most comfortable.

Wear a thin sock inside the shoe and when there are overlapping tongues, cut off the outside flap. You want as little sock cushioning between your skin and the ball as possible. Wear only a sanitary sock inside your shoe. Tie the knot of your shoe to the side, underneath, or perhaps in back of your shoe.

You need to develop a feel for the football on your foot. Passing the ball with your foot is one of the best ways to develop this sense. Try it in your room if the rest of the household has no objections. Sit on your bed and balance the ball on your foot; then pass it to a wastebasket. Fifty times a night will be a great help in developing skill that will pay off on the field.

The end-over-end punt coming off the kicking foot.

The natural kick for a right-footed kicker is the left spiral. It is easy and natural to lay the ball across your foot because of the left pointing of your right hand, which holds the ball. When the left spiral hits the ground downfield, it will bounce to the right at a 90-degree angle. But if you are a left-footed kicker and hold the ball with your left hand, your kick will be a right spiral and will bounce to the left at a 90-degree angle. Seldom have there been football kickers able to kick with both feet. We do see this ability in soccer players, but not among American kickers. It would be advantageous if you could develop into a switch kicker. Try it.

If a right-footed kicker wants to kick out of bounds to his left, it is more satisfactory to use an end-over-end kick. There is no difference in the motion for an end-over-end kick than there is in the motion for kicking a spiral. You must direct the laying of the ball on your foot so that the midseam lies on the middle of your foot in the lengthwise direction. The result is a fine end-over-end kick, a kick that spins on its short axis. Because of its bounce, this is a wonderful kick for a quick kick. The ball rotates forward and after landing may bounce along for another 25 yards or more.

This roll is far too important to be passed by without some real understanding of it.

The roll is one advantage of accurate kicking. Most coaches have not taught their safety men to handle rolling balls, and so they let them roll even if they roll toward their own goal line. These rolling balls can be handled, but lots of time must be spent practicing for the job. Few teams take the time to do it, so you have a great advantage when you kick this kind of rolling ball.

When teams kick on fourth down, they don't count on the roll. Usually they kick the ball directly to the safety man, hoping to get their team downfield to tackle him as soon as he catches the ball. You must have seen such kicks Saturdays and Sundays on TV. Because these kicks are so high, they roll very little, even when the ball is not caught. Such a kick may even roll back toward the kicker if he was off-balance when he kicked the ball. Your kicks will never do this, because you are learning to kick in a balanced position right from the start.

An accurate kick with a low trajectory, which you can accomplish, just begins to make life difficult for the safety man when it hits the ground in those wide-open spaces on the field. There are many kinds of rolls, but there are two main types:

- The roll that follows the end-over-end punt.
- The roll that follows the spiral punt.

After an end-over-end kick, the ball reaches the ground already revolving on its short axis and starts immediately to roll without loss of speed or change of direction.

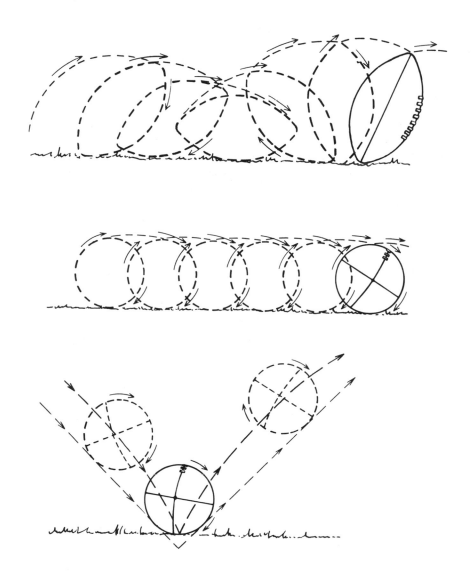

Top: The roll that follows the end-over-end punt. Center: The roll that follows the spiral punt. Bottom: The 90° bounce of a left spiral hitting the ground.

After a spiral kick, the ball reaches the ground still spiraling on it long axis and must find its way back to an end-over-end position, revolving on its short axis.

Watch a spiraling kick as it hits the ground and attempts to find an end-over-end roll. It is delayed, and its course is likely to be erratic. Its roll distance is shortened, and its course may even be altered by uneven ground. You'll always get a better, faster roll from the end-over-end kick than you will from the spiral, and I recommend much more use of the end-over-end punt than is usually made.

The speed and the distance of the roll are affected by the trajectory of the kick and the total motion of the punter from the time he starts his kicking motion until he has stopped it and his feet are on the ground without movement. Many times we have been told that when the foot has contacted the ball, everything has been decided. That is not so. When you see a punter kick a ball and during the motion his kicking foot lands behind him, you can be sure that the ball, if it hits the ground, will not roll forward but will either bounce up and down or roll back toward the kicker. If you wish a ball to roll away from you after kicking, then you have to be ready to move forward when your kicking foot strikes the ground after the kick. Try it and you'll understand the principle that "for every action there is an equal and opposite reaction."

A punt leaving the kicker at a 45 degree angle to the ground will go the farthest. The football follows a pattern of a parabola in the air and not that of a circle. The higher the angle of leaving the ground, generally the less distance. It may have great hang time but not as good distance.

More distance can be achieved in punting the football by increasing the length of your second step. There is a limitation, however, to the extent of improvement possible. The key is to maintain your balance. When the length of the step takes you off balance, then cut down the distance of the step.

When you approach the business of actually kicking the football, wear all your game equipment. Then practice takes on much of the feeling of a game's kicking situation. Don't forget those short cleats on your kicking foot, and be sure to avoid knots on the front of the shoe. Now you are ready to apply power to the football.

A good way to start is by passing the ball off your foot. Stand in your fundamental stance, place the ball on your kicking foot, and with one finger on the ball's laces, pass it about 5 yards to a teammate or the manager. Do it fifty times for an end-over-end kick. Then do it fifty times for your left spiral.

Before practicing your punting with the two step approach, try punting without a step. No-step kicking is done by standing on your balance foot with the ball held on your hip; then, as the kicking leg swings forward, place

the ball on the foot for left spiral. This is a drill to increase the speed of the leg because each time you kick, you should try to have your right heel hit you in the butt prior to swinging down and through. This motion places your quadriceps in a stretched position. For the motion, this pre-stretch tends to speed up the motion. Work on this. Try every day to kick fifty of these to each corner. It will pay off in more accurate kicking and longer punts.

Now, using steps, try some warm-up kicks of 35 or 40 yards. Then move back for some longer ones.

Next try some out-of-bounds punting. Stand on the 35 yard line at the hash mark and see if you can put some kicks out of bounds inside the five. See if you can roll some kicks out-of-bounds.

In taking your "get set" position, aim your left foot at some target high and off the field. While holding the ball properly, try stepping with your left foot, transferring all your weight to this balance foot, and moving into the kicking action with an easy flow of power. As your right leg swings forward, lay the ball across your foot well up on the instep, as you have already practiced. By extending your leg forcibly, you'll apply power to your kick. Strive for a well-depressed toe, and the ball will roll off your foot in a low trajectory that will roll it out of bounds.

Kick five times from the 20-yard line, and then move out to the 25-yard line. Kick five times there, and then move back to the 30-yard line mark. Each time you complete five successful kicks move back another 5 yards.

How to Punt the Football

The short kicks are a good warm-up for kicks 30, 35, and 40 yards. Go through this routine every day you kick, and then about once a week extend your distance to the maximum. You'll be amazed at how quickly you develop your feel for the ball on your foot and begin to kick those 40-yarders with ease.

Whenever possible in your practice kicking, have a center who will snap the ball back to you. Explain to your center that you want to receive the ball with the laces up, and have him work on delivering it that way. Then it is very easy to slide your right hand under the ball and place your middle finger under the midseam.

If no center is available, perhaps you can kick to another kicker and let him throw the ball back to you. Catch the ball, adjust it, and kick. This is good practice, too. Then you can switch roles with the other kicker.

Here is an important habit you should develop: After getting set, transfer most of your weight to your right foot. Then when you receive the snap from the center, you can simply step with your left foot and kick with your right. For kicks of up to 35 yards and all quick kicks, you'll need only that left step. (When you want to kick for longer distances, you may want to take a short step with your right foot before the left step, in order to develop momentum.)

When you kick with good balance, you'll be able to put your kicking foot down in the same relative position as it was before you kicked. At the end of every kick you should be in position to kick another football without changing your position. This is a true test of balanced kicking.

Many people have the mistaken idea that excessive force makes for good kicking. What really produces good kicks is the controlled and properly timed follow-through of the foot. The harder the football is kicked without control, the shorter the distance it will travel and the more inaccurate the result. A properly kicked punt should make very little noise. It should produce more of a swish than a thud. Try to keep your foot under the ball as long as possible each time you kick. After hundreds of practice attempts you'll get the feel of it.

One common fault in follow-through is to turn you toe up too far. This error throws the ball high and may even cause an end-over-end punt to revolve backward toward you. This reversal can easily cost you 10 to 15 yards per kick. You have seen this happen, or you will some afternoon. The TV announcers and others sometimes blame such kicks on the wind or an uneven field instead of on the kicker.

When the spiral leaves your foot, its action is very much like that of a guided missile. The distance of the kick depends not on the excessive force but on the timing and length of the follow-through. Your follow-through will be affected by your ability to depress your kicking toe. Practice every day stretching the ligaments and muscles that depress the toe on your kicking foot. As you become more skillfull with the handling of the football on your foot, you'll learn to turn your toe down when you want to release the ball for its air flight. You can kick a 30-yard punt with about one-half of a follow-through. Accurate and long punting are based on some simple learnable factors. You can have great kicking success with some intelligent planning and practice.

Always kick to a target. Remember that the balance foot is the anchor foot and also the aiming foot. It is not wise to kick a football 20 yards farther than your opponents can kick if you are not accurate. Many beautiful kicks across the goal line for a touchback and then are automatically put into play on the 20-yard line. What a waste of that "hidden yardage" you might have had with an accurate out-of-bounds kick inside the 5-yard line. Perhaps you could have downed it on the 2-yard line.

Remember another advantage of that rolling, bouncing ball is that the safety man loses his immunity from a block. If your two ends are following a rolling ball, one man can block and the other can down the ball at a point near the goal line. On the high kick, however, no one can block or touch the safety man until he has touched the ball, and he may also signal for a fair catch, a move that extends his immunity from being manhandled.

A right-footed kicker, in spite of aiming at the target with his balance foot, may find the ball goes to the left of the foot's direction. The action of kicking tends to turn your body to the left, even with the left foot anchored.

The depressed toe kick, showing the ball leaving the foot after the follow-through.

The resulting "pull" will drive the ball off target. If you have this problem, just aim to the right of the target you wish to hit. How far off the target to aim can be determined only by your practice sessions and by referring to some tests in the back of this book. This left pull holds true in place-kicking or drop-kicking by a right-footed kicker. You'll see this tendency demonstrated time and time again in football games. You can be sure that if a right-footed place kicker misses his field goal, most of the time it will pull to the left of the goalposts.

Right footed kickers also may slice their kick. This is caused in most cases by the leg crossing over to the left or because the kicker has lost his balance while kicking and the power of the swing of the kicking leg has turned his body and foot while in the process of kicking. We may also have a condition covered previously when the adductor muscles are stronger than the abductor. The sliced kick flies off to the right always out of control. When we were first taught to kick a spiral, this was the system. It was thought that you couldn't make the football spiral without kicking across the bottom of the ball as you dropped it on your foot. Now we have learned much more about kicking and know that it will spiral if laid across the ankle when being kicked.

Quite often inexperienced or untrained kickers will take their eyes off the ball and look at oncoming opponents. This takes them off balance and they drop the ball on their foot out of control. Then the foot will meet the ball to the left of its middle causing a drastic slice to the right. This happens because of the game pressure on a critical kick and the lack of training of the kicker.

You may see one of those kickers who throws the ball out ahead of him and kicks when leaping off the ground. He is apt to do some slicing of his kicks because he is way off balance when he kicks.

Goal kickers can also slice and if they do they contact the ball to the left of the midseam and the ball goes to the right of the goalposts if he is right-footed kicker.

I know of no way to be an accurate kicker if you slice. A left pull by a right-footed kicker can be corrected to some extent and can be allowed for in your aiming, but a slice is deadly. So, stay with the fundamentals that have been discussed previously in this book and you'll have no difficulty with a slice.

Once you have learned balance and direction, you must learn to estimate distance. In order to kick the distance you intend, you must learn the feel of power in your foot and leg. Learn the degrees of power by practice. Learn to ration it so you can control your kick. This feeling is known as the kinesthetic sense. You can develop your kinesthetic sense, but it takes practice and more practice. Blind people develop this sense to a much higher degree than do sighted people. It is a necessity for them.

Power application from the right side of the body can cause the ball to turn to the left.

Once you have developed some consistency in your kicking, try kicking with a blindfold on, each time trying to estimate where the ball went. At first you'll be unable to estimate very accurately, but as you work at this skill, you'll get better and better at it.

When your coach calls for a high punt, that is what you should deliver. It is simple. Hold the ball with its front point up, and lay the ball on your foot in that position. If the kick is to be a spiral, then the belly of the ball will touch your instep above where the big toe and the ankle come together. You'll also want to release the ball at about the midline of your body with your toe well depressed. If you watch some of the pro kickers, you'll notice that this kind of kick is what they do best. They use more of the front part of their foot than they do the curve of their ankle. Of course, you won't fall back after kicking. To do so would take away from the distance of your kick.

If your coach wants a low ball, tilt the front down when you lay the ball on your foot. With very little effort on your part this ball will travel about 30 yards in the air and have a very fast and long roll if you are balanced when you kick it. To speed up this roll, just start walking forward after you finish your kicking follow-through. I have seen this kind of punt travel 40 yards in the air and then roll 30 yards more. This is a devastating kick for the receiving team if it is kept away from the safety man.

In football games, the punter has
One goal for which he yearns:
He'd like his every kick to be
The punt of no return.

Dick Emmons

3
The Quick-Kick Disaster for Your Opponents

Have you ever seen a quick kick upset a football game? The success of this strategy is largely a result of its being unexpected.

The term "quick kick" comes from the situation in which the ball is kicked. It is kicked from a spot 4 to 5 yards behind the line of scrimmage through the line and over the heads of incoming linemen. It is most effective in a second-down or third-down situation when your opponents are expecting a forward pass or run. On such a play the safety man is usually close to the line of scrimmage and not ready for a kick. Most teams have a man specially trained to run back punts, but on second or third down he's not ordinarily in the game. When you kick the ball in this situation, you change the whole strategy of the game. Your opponents, tuned in for defense, suddenly find that they are the offense and, if the quick kick is well placed, have the ball in a poor position near their goal line. You can master the art of delivering a quick kick as well as you can kick an ordinary punt from punt information.

In order to take full advantage of the quick kick, you must be able to control it. This kick should be played from one of your coach's basic formations and must look like a pass or run until the moment you kick the ball.

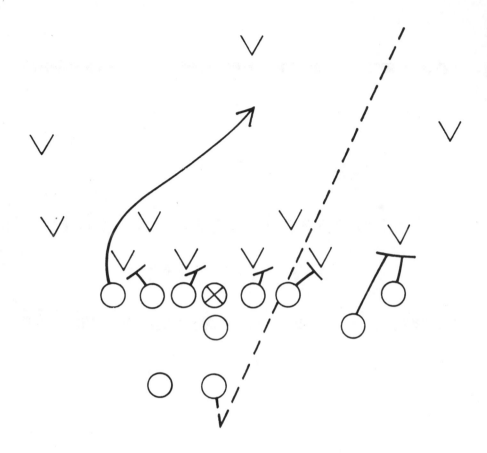

The quick-kick formation with the kicker fading back.

The quick kick is a punt, either an end-over-end or a spiral, and is kicked close to the scrimmage line from your hands low and fairly close to your body. If the safety man is near the line of scrimmage, he has no chance to get hold of the ball. After it hits the ground, it will roll for much additional yardage. Your ends will go down and follow the ball until it reaches its nearest point to the goal line and then will "kill" it there. Your opponents now take possession of the football in very poor position. Your coach may like this kind of strategy, which is known as playing position football.

You'll have no trouble with quick-kicking if you take advantage of every chance for continuous practice and thinking about balanced movement, constant aiming of the ball, proper laying of the ball on your foot, and suitable follow-through. Use the same fundamentals that are used for all kicking.

You can practice the quick-kicking fade-back steps without a center. But when you have perfected these steps, working with a center becomes very helpful. Learn to take two or four steps back before the ball is passed from center on signal, in order to put yourself in position to receive the ball and kick it.

The first step back is with your kicking foot. The second step back is with your balance foot. When this balance foot strikes the ground the ball should be snapped from center to your right knee. You, then take one step with your balance foot and kick an end-over-end punt. Kick this ball straight ahead and you'll have a very long roll.

The successful timing of this play depends on having the center put the ball into your right hand when your balance foot strikes the ground and you are in position to kick. You will take one step with your balance foot toward your target and then kick.

After kicking the ball, keep walking toward your target to assure yourself of the maximum distance of the roll. If you should be interfered with in this action, you'll probably get some penalty yardage. So move right into the walk just as soon as your kicking foot comes back to the ground.

Your quick kick can be a spiral or an end-over-end punt. The end-over-end punt will roll much farther than the spiral. The left spiral from your right foot will cut to the sideline faster if you are near the center of the field. It may cost you some distance. I recommend the end-over-end quick kick in most situations unless there is wind, because the safety man will never catch up with the roll once the ball goes over his head.

Wind currents and the condition of the field may determine what type of quick kick you'll use and where you'll place it. On a turtle-backed field your end-over-end kick will bounce toward the sideline after it starts to roll. Therefore, you may want to direct it downfield and depend on your ends to kill this roll in the best spot for your team.

When you practice the fade-back steps for the quick kick, take a bigger step with your kicking foot than with your balance foot. You will learn to adjust the length of your stride as you practice this maneuver. After a while these steps become almost automatic for you when the quick kick is called in the huddle.

In most of the game situations suitable for the quick kick, you'll want to aim for the "coffin corner." You need targets in these corners, and here is a way to pick them.

Have someone stand on a 5-yard line while you stand on the same side of the field facing him on the hash mark at the 50-yard line. Sight down to your man on the 5-yard line, and try to find something high above him to aim for (a pole is ideal). Or maybe there will be an exit or entrance sign in a stadium. Don't pick a flag down on the field, because it may be obscured by players or spectators standing in front of it during the game. Pick targets for yourself in the four corners, and be ready for your kicking assignment.

Rarely have I seen a quick kick blocked, even when the team that was using it had been widely heralded as a quick-kicking team. Usually the move is such a surprise to a defensive team that the ball has been kicked and is away before the defense wakes up to the strategy.

The quick kick, of course, is not a fourth-down play, and you don't try it then.

If your coach is quick-kick-conscious, he will probably have a good pass play, which you should know very well, designed to look like your quick-kick formation. The quick kick is especially successful with the wind at your back, but not very good if you are facing the wind.

Practice your fade-back steps every day. When you have your center working with you, have him concentrate on trying to place the ball so that it comes to you with laces up and opposite your left knee. Sometimes work with an end and see if you can throw a forward pass to him on his outside. This maneuver makes a good companion play to the quick kick on the second down. Such a pass is very effective as a surprise play to use after you have gotten a reputation as a quick kicker. Football is a game of head, hands, and feet. Every type of legal strategy should be used.

Your coach will be the judge of when your team uses the quick kick. But you can be ready, and you can demonstrate that you know the technique. He'll be pleased to know that he has a player with this skill. Few coaches have enough time to make their kickers as good as they would like them. Most coaches must rely on a certain amount of self-teaching by their kickers.

For several years the quick kick was rarely used. But as the defense has been crowding in on the offense, more coaches have realized the advantage of using this kick as a part of their strategy to improve field position. You'll rarely see this kick used on first down, but mainly on second and third down, and never on fourth down. There is a great advantage in making your opponents play their offense near their own goal line, and the quick kick can accomplish this.

Because the quick kick depends so much upon the team play of you and the center, the two of you need to practice together at every possible opportunity. Help him to get the ball to you with laces up and on target above your right knee and opposite your left knee.

The football is actually propelled better when the laces are up; the smooth belly of the ball gives better contact with your ankle. Plastering a piece of adhesive tape across your shoelaces is a help in making the ankle smooth.

The Quick-Kick Disaster for Your Opponents

A successful quick kick requires that you get into a balanced position with your left foot (the balance-anchor-directional foot) aimed for your kick. In the huddle, start to aim yourself toward one of those targets you selected before the game began. Then, when you're in position, lay the ball on your foot and kick it with an easy follow-through. Keep right on walking down toward the target to see how many yards you can put into the roll.

If you want to work on improving your follow-through, take off your shoe and kick with your bare foot or with just a sock. This will stop your tendency to slap the ball. There is an instinctive action to protect your foot that will prevent a slap, and you'll increase your follow-through, thereby increasing the time that your foot stays under the ball.

Your kicking success depends to a great extent on your *thinking* kicking every extra minute you can devote to it, just as being good in any other endeavor requires similar concentration. Your foot obeys commands that are given to it from your brain.

Holding the ball for a drop kick, with the kicking leg at the ready.

4
Scoring Kicks, Drop Kicks, and Place Kicks

A drop kick is a kick in which the ball is dropped from your hands to the ground and kicked the instant it rises from the ground. Its variations include the high-trajectory, the low-trajectory (for distance), the rapid-revolving, and the slow-revolving (or floating) kicks. The slow-revolving drop kick carries best for distance.

You can learn the drop kick easily, even though it isn't widely used today. You'll surprise many people because they don't know that it is legal to drop-kick for goals, kickoffs, and free kicks. Drop-kicking is not too difficult, and you make use of the basic fundamentals I have already mentioned in connection with other kicks.

Some coaches say that it is a waste of time to teach drop-kicking. They say the ball is too narrow. Actually the size of the approved collegiate football has not changed since 1934. If it is too narrow for the drop kick, why isn't it too narrow for the place kick?

You can drop-kick a football just as easily as you can place-kick it accurately. You must, however, be sure to drop the ball accurately so that it will bounce straight up. Today's football is easier to slice or hook than was the old wide pre-1934 ball, but the problem is no greater in the drop kick than it is in the place kick. The modern ball is also lighter than was the old-fashioned model, and this difference is an advantage for today's kicker.

Learning to drop this ball and have it bounce straight up is easier than you might think. If a forty-five-year-old man with ordinary street shoes can do it, so can you. The famous Charlie Brickley of Harvard fame did this at my New York World's Fair Kicking School. The same day his two sons demonstrated similar ability and put on a family drop-kicking contest. They merely demonstrated the fundamentals covered in the previous pages in this book. In England, Rugby players think nothing of drop-kicking on the run to make points. They do have a wider ball, but it is also heavier and therefore requires a slightly different kicking skill. But all that drop-kicking does serve to demonstrate is that the feat is possible.

The English use a somewhat different technique from ours. They use the whole ankle. This is what we call a basket boot, and I have taught some kickers to use it successfully. Today's soccer type of placement kickers also use the whole ankle in a sort of basket kick. For some kickers this is a very natural and successful way to kick.

I believe that one of the best ways to learn drop-kicking is to start by standing on your balance foot and bending your kicking foot behind your

The kicker keeps his eyes on the ball, and does not "sneak a peek" elsewhere.

knee. Hold the ball with two hands very close to the ground. Then drop the ball in front of your kicking foot, and when the ball bounces, kick it.

This is what used to be called a pendulum boot and was one way that points after touchdown were kicked. They still could be. After you get skillful at this fundamental drop-kicking, you can go on to drop-kicking with a step.

You'll have very little difficulty with drop-kicking or place-kicking when you have become comfortable and skillful in the fundamentals. A little more detail will help you in point scoring.

Your timing is even more important in kicking for points than it is in punting. In the drop kick your foot must meet the ball at just the right instant as it bounces from the ground. Your toe should hit a spot 3 or 4 inches from the point of the ball. If the ball is held vertically and kicked, it will be good for the point after touchdown.

A kick timed very quickly spins too fast and will not go very far. A ball kicked too slowly or timed too slowly is not likely to look like a drop kick at all and will resemble a punt.

For your point-after-touchdown attempts, the ball, whether you drop-kick or place-kick it, must be kicked from the vertical position. Eventually you'll be able to hit the right spot with your toe every time.

There is one best way to drop the ball for drop-kicking. Start by holding the ball in two hands over the right foot as close to the ground as possible. One hand is on each side of the ball, and each middle finger is on a side seam just below the center of the ball. Rest your thumbs on the sides of the ball about an inch from the top, where some footballs have white lines. Let your fingers fall into place with your wrists about 7 inches apart. This is the width of a football. Now let your wrists relax, and you have a good hold on the ball for dropping. Do it the same way every time.

How the ball is held for the drop kick.

Holding the ball this way gives you steadiness and accurate placement of the ball in front of your kicking foot. Bend over and drop the ball as near the ground as you can; the nearer, the better. Your first step is with your balance foot. Then you drop the ball and kick it on the first bounce. The ball should be dropped to the ground as nearly parallel as possible to the left knee. For longer distances than required for the point after touchdown, you drop the ball a little farther in front of your kicking foot and with a backward lean to it.

This backward lean is also necessary in the place kick for longer distances. This tilt results in a lower trajectory because your toe hits the ball a greater distance from the ground. Such a kick gives you a slower spin and a longer distance from the same power. You will be kicking the ball about 4½ inches from the point.

To give you a spot on which to focus, measure five inches from the point of the football and make a mark on the seam. Draw a circle 1 inch in diameter here and color it red. Then, draw a triangle around this circle, about 2 inches on a side, point down. When you go out to kick, take some soft chalk and chalk the circle. After you kick this ball, look to see if you have chalk on your toe. Another way to check up is to chalk your kicking toe and examine your ball after kicking it. The chalk will leave a mark on the ball. Check the ball each time after kicking and then compare your performance on each of the kicks. For a high kick, your toe should be hitting the point of the triangle. For the longer kick with slower rotation, your toe should be hitting the base of the triangle.

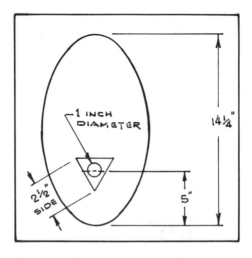

When your toe hits the ball, your ankle should be locked in almost a right-angle position. This is a part of the secret of delivering the power to the ball. Another tip: I have all my right-footed kickers aim for the right goalpost because of their natural left pull. This pull brings the ball inside the goalposts.

I have asked many kickers who didn't know me what they aim at when kicking goals. Surprisingly many have said, "The middle of the goalposts." This idea is confusing; there is no middle marked anywhere on the crossbar except for the center support. That is a poor target because it does not extend above the crossbar.

Try to find a vertical target that is above the crossbar and just inside the right upright. It gives your eyes an opportunity to follow up its height and helps you aim and your kick. If there is no such target available, maybe there is a corner of the stadium or numbered exit that you can use just as you did with the punt.

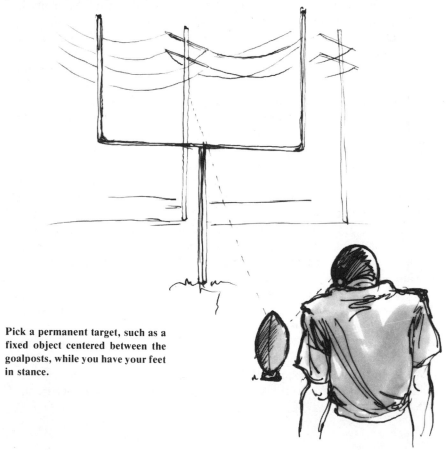

Pick a permanent target, such as a fixed object centered between the goalposts, while you have your feet in stance.

Some years ago, one of my college kickers picked out a girl with a red dress for his target when we were spotting targets before the game. I suggested that she might move during the game and he would have no target. Pick a permanent target inside the right upright somewhere behind the posts.

There is room for about forty footballs side by side between the goalposts. You don't have to be exactly a sharpshooter to get the ball between them. But if you're off-balance or sneak a look at the incoming linemen, the ball will veer off that left upright, caused by your pull.

Try to put the ball somewhere between the two uprights. To get it there, you will have to aim to the right of the imaginary center. Keep checking your targets. When you miss a kick, try to figure out why. Keep your head down and your eyes on the ball. That's the way to kick it through.

Except for dropping the ball, the place kicker depends on the same routine as the drop kicker. Whichever of these kicks you deliver, you should recover your balance and finish up with your kicking foot on the ground in the same relative position as when you started to kick.

It seems to me that the drop kick is superior to the place kick except on wet and muddy days. Why? The drop kick:

1. Can be learned as easily as, or perhaps more easily than, a place kick.
2. Can be as accurate as a place kick, as quick as a place kick.
3. Releases an extra player for block (almost reason enough in itself).
4. Can be gotten away better than a place kick after a bad pass from center. Less liable to be blocked, because it is kicked from a greater distance behind the line of scrimmage.

Practice both place kicks and drop kicks. Someday surprise your coach by drop-kicking one between the uprights from an angle about 20 yards away using an easy motion and complete follow-through.

When some of the professional place kickers step up to the ball and make those Sunday kicks, it sure looks easy, doesn't it? One of their secrets is concentration. Concentration on their whole skill makes these successes possible.

But when they miss some easy ones, you wonder why. I watched a Miami Dolphin kicker miss one from 14 yards away and was amazed. The ball did hit the left goalpost, so I knew his left pull had taken the ball over there. Maybe he peeked at those rushing linemen. If so, he couldn't have been concentrating on kicking.

When all the basic fundamentals are working together for the practiced kicker, his job is easy. So if you want to become a good place kicker, start with the fundamentals.

The ankle is the apex of the 90° angle of foot and leg when the toe contacts the ball for a place kick.

First you should realize that when you place-kick, your balance-anchor-directional foot must be beside the ball with your weight on it. This is true whether you use just one step or one step and one-half. Take your stance facing the ball so that all you need to do is shift your weight to your kicking foot (which is in front of your balance foot), and then firmly place your *balance* foot (left for right-footed kickers) so that its toe is about 4 inches behind the side seam of the ball and about 4 inches to the left of the ball. Now swing your kicking leg with your eyes on the ball, watching to see the toe meet it.

In order to get maximum distance, you must have a follow-through that is easy and complete. By lifting your left arm, you can help your right leg follow-through. Why? Because we still behave as though we were four-footed. You'll notice that any animal normally walks by placing its left front foot forward when its right rear leg goes forward. Our arms and legs work with the diagonally opposite member.

When your foot has stopped pushing the ball, you should have control enough that you can place your kicking foot back onto the ground in the spot where the ball stood before you kicked it. If you can do this, you are well balanced.

In performing the place kick, you must depend on an element that is not involved in the punt of the drop kick. It's the ball holder. He has the job of receiving the ball from the center and then placing it down for you to kick. Many coaches have a gadget that consists of a tee attached to two cross tapes. This setup is for planning the direction of the kick and indicating the spot where the ball will be placed for kicking. This cross is usually placed from 6 to 7 yards behind the line of scrimmage. On the long part of the tape, the kicker usually has his steps marked off.

If your coach has one of these gadgets, try pointing it at the right goalpost. Kick in that direction to determine how much pull you have as a right-footed kicker. Have one of your teammates watch the kicks and tell you how far inside the posts you are kicking when aiming at the right post. If your coach doesn't have one of these crossed-tape affairs, you can make one out of adhesive tape or tennis tape.

Teach the man who holds the ball for you to hold the top of the ball with *four* fingers and not just one. This method makes it possible for him to be more certain of holding the ball straight up and down rather than leaning it to either side. He can also rotate the ball quickly and get the laces where they belong, away from your toe and facing the goalposts.

Try having your ball holder squat rather than kneel. If he's squatting, he has a better chance to handle a poor pass from center. Another possibility of this position is for him to catch the ball, fake a kick, and then pass. Some coaches, however, will prefer to have your holder kneel on his right knee and place his left foot on the ground. They believe this is a steadier position.

To place-kick the point after touchdown, you need to take only one step with your balance foot and then swing your kicking leg. That kind of kick will send the ball 20 to 25 yards if you follow-through.

Here's the sequence: In your "get set" position shift your weight to your kicking foot; then take a left step, lean back, and kick. Control your foot, and bring it down to the same relative position it was in when you started to kick. You should then be standing in your original kicking stance. Keep looking down until your foot has finished the kick and is back down on the ground.

In moving toward the ball, you must always have your feet parallel whether you use one step or one step and a half. Then concentrate on kicking the ball at just the right spot on the seam.

When you practice place-kicking, you must have someone hold the ball for you, tee it up, or dig a hole in the ground to hold it. Setting it up is a very good practice because you can adjust the tilt of the ball for short or long kicks.

For the point-after-touchdown kick, the ball should be straight up and down. You can scratch out a cross with your cleats for kicking the point after touchdown.

Try a point about 10 yards back from the goal line. You know that in a game the ball will be put into play by the center from the 2-yard line. This will give him an 7-yard pass, which is a safe distance.

Stand beside the ball after you have set it up, and try kicking without a step. This is fine practice exercise for follow-through. If you have a younger brother or friend, perhaps he'll chase some balls for you and tell you about your accuracy.

After you have begun doing very well in front of the goalpost, move several yards to the side and try. Finally do some kicking from the sidelines. This variety will help your accuracy. You'll also find out a great deal about your left pull. Try to place your left foot so that you never get any feeling of reaching for the ball with your kicking foot. You see this sort of thing happen to many kickoff men, and it spoils their kick.

For kicks up to 35 yards you'll need only one step, so try kicking by merely stepping with your balance foot. You'll have to use a complete follow-through to get distance. Never fall into the habit of punching the ball with your foot. This way of kicking throws off your balance and your accuracy. Before you step with your left foot, you may want consciously to transfer your weight to the kicking foot. That procedure may work better for you.

When you have developed your skill enough that you want to try 40-yard kicks, you may want to take a short step with your kicking foot before the step with your balance-anchor-directional foot. This skill must be practiced until the swing of your leg, the locking of your ankle, and your toe hitting the ball where you want it to all become automatic.

Most difficult of all is *keeping your eye on the ball* while so many distracting sights and sounds are going on. That is the way your opponents will try to block your kick or spoil it. Be ready for all that noisemaking at the scrimmage line when you kick.

You may have set up a routine for yourself on the field. If you have no kicking coach, each day start your place-kicking from 10 yards back on the sideline. A leg must be warmed up like an arm. Aim at the right goalpost and kick. If this is too far for you, move in toward the goalposts. Kick three tries through the goalposts.

As soon as you have done this, move back and do three more. After each successful three attempts, move back until you have found your limit. If you miss, move up until you succeed. The 30-yard angle will probably be the most difficult for you. At that distance the goalposts look close together and far away. But when you get into a game, they'll never be so close together and your kicking will be much easier.

Don't underestimate the importance of aiming. Some days you'll have to compensate for the wind, as well as for your natural pull and maybe for a tendency to lift off your balance heel. Remember that the best targets are telephone poles or other vertical objects. Get a look at your target from the huddle. When you come out to kick, plant your directional foot in your "get set" position. When the ball comes from center, take your step, keep your eye down, and kick. The roar of the crowd will tell you that your kick was good. You don't have to peek. Don't.

If there is ever a day when your kicks and your timing seem to be off, go back to the fundamentals. Pass the ball off your foot for punting, or try

The place kick is executed with the balance foot practically alongside the ball.

some drop kicks or place kicks without taking any steps. Just stand on your balance foot, bend your right leg back of your knee, and drop-kick a short one with good follow-through. Move back to 15, and every time you succeed, move back 5 yards. If you have a bad kick, then move up 5 yards. This planned practice will do more for you than any other kind of kicking that I know about.

Start thinking positive: Your kicks will succeed; you can control that football. Say to yourself, "That ball will go through the goalposts."

Most successful people develop their confidence through hard work and experience. So can you. If you make mistakes, think back to the fundamentals of all kicking.

That balance-anchor-directional foot will be to blame for most difficulties you ever have with kicking. As long as that foot is flat and pointing at your target, your kicks will go where you want them to. Get the habit of walking and putting your left heel down when you take that step.

Become aware of the wind and its power. Someday you'll have to adjust to it on the field. Watch kites when they are flying. Notice how strongly paper will rise with the wind blowing across it. A football will behave similarly. Never kick directly into the wind. Always plan to kick as much as possible across it.

The soccer style of place kicking has come into vogue in football during the past few years.

5

The Soccer Type Placekick

In the early seventies the football world was amazed when two young Hungarians burst on the Ivy League scene to kick field goals soccer style. The Gogolak brothers started a new trend for kicking of field goals which has gained followers every year so that now there are more soccer type field goal kickers in the pro leagues than the conventional straight-on type of field goal kickers.

Everywhere in countries where soccer is played, young boys develop great foot dexterity by their constant "footing" or kicking a round ball up and down the streets and on the fields near their homes. While this has been going on, the American boy has been spending a great deal of his time throwing and catching, batting or shooting baskets. All of these activities are making him an expert in hand arm and dexterity. So, it is evident it will take more time for an American boy to develop foot dexterity to compete with the Europeans. It is happening, however, because of the erupting growth of the game of soccer on playgrounds and fields all over America. Many small high schools have given up football for soccer. This is due partly to the high cost of football and partly to the increased interest in soccer.

The soccer type field goal kicker is here to stay. So, how do you do it? It is a kick that will be done with the ball on the ground and in most cases either held by a holder or by setting it on a tee. It can also be drop-kicked.

Place kicks for extra points or field goals can very well be called the "game within the game" performed by the "team within a team." This concept of the "team within a team" is a creation of my friend and colleague, Mike Rendina, who has developed the best high school kicker in the nation, his son, Mike Rendina, Jr.

When the point after touchdown is required, the eleven men who come on the field to kick a field goal or kick the extra points are frequently referred to collectively as a "special team." This "team within a team" could very well be called the super-special team.

The team within the team consists of three men—the center, the ball holder and the kicker. You, as the kicker, cannot be successful if these other members of your team do not perform well. There should be a lot of time spent in working out this team effort.

Your holder should take a position in which his left knee is on the ground and his right foot extended toward the center to help the center align the football into the hands of the holder.

You should expect that your holder will take a position in which his left knee is on the ground and his right foot extended toward the center to help the center align the ball into the hands of the holder. In most cases the holder will be a quarterback because he is more skilled in handling the ball than anybody except the center. A second string center should also make a very good holder for you or a wide receiver.

It is the responsibility of the holder to place the ball on the tee without leaning the ball sidewards, forward or back. In order to assist the holder, a spot can be painted on the black tee. You, the kicker, can focus on this spot and your holder can place the ball on it every time in exactly the same place.

The holder should "hold" the ball with his right first finger.

57

At impact, your body should come to a straight up position over the ball.

When the ball comes to the holder, you should expect that he will catch it in his two hands and that the right hand will feel for the laces while his left hand is rotating the ball to give you, the kicker, a ball on the tee with the laces away from you. This should be done before the ball is placed on the tee. Nothing is as confusing as to have a holder spin the ball on the tee while you are starting your approach to the ball. The ball will be held with his right first finger on top, or I like to use four fingers. The left hand must be well out of the way when the kick starts. Accurate placement of the ball on the tee is a guarantee to you that you will not have to make any final adjustments after you start your move toward the ball for your kick. Most slices and pulls are the result of poor placement of the ball on the tee.

Now, what should you be doing as a soccer style kicker? It is up to you to see that your tee is placed correctly and aimed at where you want the ball to go. Don't leave it up to your holder. After making a determination of the wind situation and your own possible pull, you can place the tee aimed for where you want the ball to go. This will be at a point about 7 yards from the ball when it is placed for the field goal or extra point.

For beginning soccer style kickers, we should suggest that you start at the ball and take two steps back and then two steps to the left. This will give you a position with a 45 degree approach to the ball. Start with your kicking foot back. Assuming you are a right footed kicker, your approach to the ball will start with the plant foot, or your left foot. When you have completed your approach to the ball, your plant foot should be even with the front of the ball and you swing your kicking foot around in an arc that brings your ankle in contact with the ball. The swinging motion of the kicking foot must be in line with the intended ball direction. Additionally, the firmness of the plant foot on the ground is very important or foot velocity will be lost. The placement of the plant foot, depending on each individual kicker, can vary from four to eight inches to the left of the kicking tee. Because the angle of flight will differ from the right or left, targeting must be adapted to correlate with different field positions. Generally we have found that if a right footed kicker will aim at the right upright he will usually pull the ball into the middle.

When you are back in position to execute your kick, you should be relaxed and your first two steps should exhibit this condition. You need speed of movement but it can be relaxed speed. Your concentration should be on the spot on the tee. By means of your peripheral vision, you will see the ball as it starts from the center's hands.

It is not difficult to follow the ball during its travel to the holder. When you see the ball start, you should push down with your back foot and be ready to move when you see the ball on the tee. Your body will be a little forward as you start and when you plant your left foot for the readiness of the kicking foot to swing through. Your body will come to a straight-up position over the ball at impact. Many kickers lose impact because their body is leaning over the ball at impact and they do not get the amount of thrust that is possible.

For practice, make use of a ball with a design on it to help you. Take a football, measure five inches from the point and paint a one inch circle there. Then paint around it a triangle two inches on a side with the point of the triangle down. For field goals inside the 50 yard line, your ankle should contact the ball at the middle of the circle. For longer kicks the contact should be at the top of the triangle. This can be determined by chalking the circle and observing the chalk left on the foot after the contact. This is what we call your explosive contact point.

If one observes soccer type kickers, you will see many who seem not to be able to control the foot and body after the ball is kicked. This is of course part of the complete kicking motion and affects the accuracy of the kick. After contact with the ball, the kicking foot should land in front of the ball position. If the landing is over to the left, it may be that the plant foot was too far behind the line of the ball or there was a lack of control of the foot and leg.

Some kickers make use of the ankle more than the side of the foot. However, those who make use of the side of the foot and get good contact with the cuneiform bones seem to get the best kick. This gives a rigid blow to a flexible ball. The result is a ball that leaves the foot at twice the speed of the foot. After all, kicking the football is a collision. It is also a transfer of momentum from the whole body to the leg and foot. Speed is most essential to be the great kicker that you would like to be.

Kicking a football involves an explosive collision.

How about practice? After you do your stretching every day and some jogging, start your practice with some no-step kicks. Just set up the ball with some kind of holder and kick without taking a step. You should be able to kick the ball twenty-five to thirty yards just standing and swinging your leg. When you do this, try to draw your leg back so that you kick yourself in the "butt." This gives your leg muscles a pre-stretch movement and makes them react much faster when they swing the leg through. Do at least 100 kicks each day by this method. Get to work on the Plyometrics which have been discussed in another part of this book. Save your great efforts for distance to about once a week. Don't plan to kick at all the day before a game or the day after.

The kickoff is a very important part of the game of football. It sets the stage for the game. It is perhaps more important than most people believe. The kicking team has an advantage in any game. In an even-up game the kicking team has twice the chance of a touchdown on scoring its first possession than does the receiving team. Yet we see many, many teams, if given the choice, elect to receive the ball. The reasons for this are many. The team with the ball will always have difficulties with fumbles, interceptions and broken plays. This is especially true at the beginning of the game. So, you can understand why your kickoff can be very important and may be the little extra that wins the game.

If the kicking team can make the receiving team start the game behind the twenty yard line, then we consider the kickoff to be a great kick. Ideally, a good kick for the kickoff would make a receiver catch the ball in the right corner. That is because most receivers are right handed and this makes them catch the ball on their left side. They cannot run as well to the left and if they start up the right side they are to close to the sideline and should be easily covered. Few coaches seem to understand this and instruct their kickers to kick the ball down the middle.

The kickoff is quite similar to the field goal effort although you build up more momentum before your foot strikes the ball and therefore it goes further. Additionally, the ball is placed on a tee which makes it possible to get a higher trajectory, resulting in what is commonly referred to by coaches as "hang time." There seems to be many ways of getting this greater momentum for the kickoff. Some kickers use five steps, some use seven. What is most important is that when you get to the last three steps, they must be of maximum speed possible and that the plant foot lands flat beside the ball for propelling the kicking foot. Coming up to the ball the kicker should have a 15 degree lean. When his foot contacts the ball the body and his center of gravity is over the ball. This guarantees that the kicker's weight is being transferred to the kicking of the ball. Here again, when the ball is kicked, your body should have lost its momentum and have transferred it to the ball.

Coming up to the ball, the kicker should have a 15° lean.

It is my hope that no coach asks that you go down field with the wave of the special team. The function of your effort is to kick the ball and then be a safety man.

Whether you decide to be a soccer type kicker or a straight-on type, certain fundamentals seem to be universal. Balance, aiming, eye on the ball, follow-through and certain concentrations are basic. This chapter has presented the fundamentals of kicking the football in "side-winder" style or, as some people like to call it, the European way. However, when you're successful, it will make no difference how you kick this prolate spheroid. To achieve success, you will need the dedication to motivate you to kick a few thousand footballs. When you have kicked over 100,000 footballs, you will really know what the skill is all about and will begin to become a master of field goal kicking. For team success you will need the cooperation of your coach to bring together the "team within a team" and provide them with the necessary practice time together, so that working together becomes automatic.

6
Looking at the World Upside Down Your Center

Your center is part of the kicking team and starts the whole procedure for every kick except the kickoff and free kicks. If he doesn't snap the ball to you just he way you want it, you'll have some trouble. You can, however, get your kick off even after a bad pass from center because you know how to make up for these difficulties. Your training up to this point almost guarantees successful kicks. Nevertheless, you can help your center improve his play by offering a few suggestions.

Because the defense knows that your center is most important, they'll have stunts and plays aimed at him in an attempt to make his snaps from center as bad as they can. This you should expect, and so should he. This is not a book on center play, yet we cannot neglect this important phase of the kicking game.

Your center has a stance that has to be balanced, just like yours. If he isn't well balanced, your opponents can pull him forward or push him back and run men up through his position to bother you. You and he must be tuned to the same timing so that he will get the ball to you when and where you expect it.

Centering is nothing but forward-passing upside down. Some men do it easily and work from this upside-down position very well. They seem to have a feeling for it. You can explain to your center that you want three types of snaps: (1) the type that will carry back about 12 yards, to where you will be standing for your punts, and (2) the soft type for your quick kick, about 5 yards and (3) the type that will carry the ball 7 yards for placekicks.

For the long (punt) pass, he should let his arms go all the way through his legs and release the ball as far back as possible with a smooth motion.

For the short (quick kick) pass, tell him that you want the ball to come to you softly with the laces up at about hip height over your right knee. It may

The best and quickest way for a kicker to get the ball for a punt is to have it centered with a fast spiral.

take some trial-and-error work to show him how to do this. He'll have to shift his hands until he finds the grip that will give the ball to you with the laces up. Explain to him that you want to get the ball when your balance-anchor foot hits the ground. This routine will take some practice and planning before you achieve smooth execution. The time to get this sequence down pat is in your early days of practice. Then go through the motions every day.

For the fourth-down punt, you'll be back about 15 yards in order to guarantee against a blocked punt. At that distance no lineman should be near you when you kick. With little or no difficulty you'll kick the ball within the two seconds that most kicking coaches allow. In other words, from the time the center starts the ball to you, no more than two seconds should elapse before the ball is in the air.

To avoid fumbling with the ball, have the center pass it to you so that it comes to your right hand at your right hip. As a guide to your center you'll hold your hands out palms down and give him a sort of roof to pass under. As soon as you get the ball, you'll find the bottom seam with your middle finger, lay the ball on your foot, and send it on its way.

If the pass from center travels too far to your side, move over and get it. Then get back into your kicking stance for kicking. Never reach for a misdirected ball while trying to keep your position. Doing so is almost sure to result in a fumble. In practice, your coach should throw you some bad balls to get you accustomed to catching them and then jumping back into your kicking stance. Such practice will help you adjust to possible errors of a center who is under great pressure.

After you have been kicking awhile, you'll develop some peculiarities of stance and kicking. Your center and you should work out any little differences in the weeks of practice before your first game. The job should be cooperative, and the more he understands what you are trying to do, the more successful you'll be. So tell him all about it. In fact, have him try some kicking. That is the best way to make him aware of your needs as a kicker.

The best and quickest way for you to get the ball in a punt situation is to have it centered with a fast spiral. The spiral comes into your hands on the ball's long axis and allows you to cradle it and get the middle finger of your right hand on the bottom easily. You'll find that most centers pass a ball that rotates one and one-half times for every 5 yards that it travels coming back to you. In working with your center, you can adjust the way he holds the ball so that he may give it to you with the laces up.

You should have your eye on the ball as it spirals from the center into your right hand. Then your left hand will fall on to the ball naturally. There may be a little variation in the speed with which different centers pass the ball back, so try to work with all of them. Then when you get into a game, you'll know what to expect.

If you and a center expect to be sent into a game together for a punt, try to have him pass some balls to you on the sideline just before you go in.

If you have the good fortune to be playing with an intelligent and skillful center, you may want to experiment with an end-over-end pass from center for your drop kick or place kick.

Successful place-kicking depends on the teamwork of three men; your center, your holder, and you, the kicker. The three of you must work together with a definite plan for making this play. The system of having the holder indicate when he wants the ball seems to be the best way of signaling for a pass from center. The holder can use a verbal signal or hand signal. Some indication should be given to the rest of the team in the huddle on when the ball will be passed. Because your teammates just hold their positions on this kick and do not charge, the starting signal is not as important to them on a place kick as it is on a quick kick.

Most coaches like to have the center make a spiral pass to the ball holder and have it come to him so that he can get both hands on the ball without reaching. It is most important for the man doing the holding to place the ball on the spot you have indicated. You will be looking there at that spot and getting ready to kick from it. (There are disadvantages in using the kicking tee; I try to have my players kick without it for points after touchdown and even the long ones.)

The holder catches the ball and then puts it down vertically with his four fingers on top.

You start your movement as soon as you see the ball in you holder's hands and don't wait until it is placed on the ground. Keep your eyes on the placement spot until the ball covers it, and then focus on the place on the ball that you will kick. By now you have practiced your approach so much that you'll automatically put the balance foot about 4 or 5 inches behind the side seam and about the same distance from the side of the ball. If you take your steps and swing your right leg parallel to your left leg, then that ball will go between those uprights.

7

The Kickoff and the Recovery Kick (The On-Side Kick)

Let me take you in imagination to England to watch a somewhat different brand of football. The English really make a *football* game out of it. You see someone running with the ball, and then all of a sudden he kicks it. An opposing player catches it and kicks it back. This return kick is an every-other play in the game of Rugby. Rugby is the ancestor of our American football.

The Rugby football is wider than ours. It is perhaps a little easier to kick, but it does not carry so far or so accurately. Our football, however, can be kicked by a man on the run. Such a kick is just a matter of practicing the fundamentals that have been detailed earlier in this book.

If your coach is as interested in position play as he is in having possession of the football, he'll recognize the importance of the running kick in getting to a better position on the field. It is generally true that the football may be kicked anytime a player has possession of it on the field. Obviously there are times when there would be no advantage in kicking it. But at times when your whole team is in front of you, a long kick down the field would give your opponents the ball in a situation that would be most difficult; on their own 5-yard line, for instance.

One good reason for learning to kick on the run is that it is very good practice for other kicking. You can never tell when the skill will come in handy.

You have seen bad passes from center to a kicker on fourth down. When this happens, you also see kickers go back to get the ball and try to kick while in motion. Some succeed, and some do not. If they have practiced this kick-on-the-run skill, they are prepared. It is possible for a punt to be made by a flanker back who takes a pass from the man who is standing back in the long punt formation. Wouldn't this play fake out the opposition?

Here's how you learn to kick on the run.

With the ball in your right hand and close to your body and hip, start walking and say to yourself, "kicking foot, balance foot, kicking foot, balance foot," and so on. Move a little faster, and then when you say "kicking foot," kick the ball. Practice every day. Start slowly, and then speed it up.

To be successful with this kick, you must keep the ball low and lay it on your kicking foot opposite to the knee of your balance foot. (It is even possible to drop-kick on the run.)

How the ball is held, carried, and kicked for the spiral punt.

In kicking on the run, you must be well balanced on that left foot, which is still your balance-anchor-directional foot. You must keep your eye on the ball and lay the ball on your foot. Complete the follow-through of your kick before continuing to run. By walking along and following the kick, you will produce a longer roll. And you can stop a roll by falling back on your follow-through.

Spirals are easier to kick on the run, but you can also kick an end over end. Try some running kicks every day along with your regular routine. The practice will help all your kicking skills.

The Kickoff and the Recovery Kick

Kickoffs by most teams go straight down the field. Many times the ball goes over the goal line and is brought out 20 yards to be put into play. If the kicking team is behind, however, it may use what the announcers call an onside kick. Then there is a scramble for the ball.

The straight story on all this is that *every* kickoff is an onside kick. The kicking team may recover any kicked ball that has traveled 10 yards.

There will be changes on the kickoff. More teams will be kicking from the hash marks instead of from the center of the field. You can learn to make use of the geometry of the field by arranging your kicks to take advantage of the many rules of the game.

If you send the kickoff straight down the field, the average runback for high school teams is to the 30-yard line, for the college teams to the 26-yard line, and for professionals to the 22-yard line. Every receiving team has a play that is based on running back the ball that is kicked down the center of the field. Why should you kick it to them in just the way they are expecting? You can upset this strategy by using a different kind of kickoff. Kick to the right corner.

The rules allow you to drop-kick or place-kick on the kickoff. A strong case can be made for the drop kick, but let's suppose that you are going to place-kick. Look over the receiving team and notice on the basis of scouting reports where they have placed their best runner. You ordinarily don't want to kick the ball to him. If, however, he is in the corner of the field to your right, you may want to kick to him there or to the other receiver in the opposite corner. (The reason for kicking the kickoff to the right corner is that most men are right handed. There is only one left handed man in every one hundred. That means that when you kick to the right corner, these men will have to catch the ball on their left side. They will have to start up the sideline to their left. This is much more difficult than as if they were running from the right side.) Of course, you may finally decide not to kick to either of them but to put it down the middle.

You can now also go for the onside kick or what I would like to call the recovery kick. There are many onside kicks, of course. There is the one that you kick after a fair catch or after a safety. Anytime a whole team is behind the ball when it is kicked, it is an onside kick.

Try this: Set up the ball on the right hash mark for you as a right-footed kicker. If you were going to drop-kick, you would stand there. Plan to kick across the field to a point about 10 yards behind the linemen who are up front and ahead of the end who is usually standing on that other sideline.

Try to kick the ball so that it will land and not go out of bounds. To accomplish this you'll step up to the ball and kick a low-trajectory kick with good follow-through and then fall back away from the ball with two or three steps backward. This technique will "kill" the roll. For this play, your coach will probably assign certain players to go downfield and block and most likely will select your fastest man to recover the ball. This is a sensible onside kick with some real chance of recovery.

In order to confuse the opponents, another supposed kicker will line up with you and run toward the ball as if he were going to kick it but will turn off as he gets to it and let you do the kicking. Why use the right hash mark? Because of that natural pull to the left by a right-footed kicker. The left pull would then pull the ball toward your own team and help make a recovery more likely than if you were kicking with your natural pull pulling the ball away from your own team.

On this recovery kick the reason for a very low trajectory is to get the ball there fast. To deliver such a kick, you'll lean the ball back. Proper practice will have shown you how much to lean it back to put the ball just where you want it. When you have the second man in on your kicking, your opponents cannot tell until the last instant which man will kick. Your teammate could conceivably kick the ball straight down the field to one of the safety men.

In setting up your team's play for the recovery kick, suggest to your coach that he have the second man in from the sideline as the assigned recovery man. That would be his only job on the kickoff. You could then practice this kick with him many days before you ever use it.

I suggest that the first man in from the sideline be assigned to blocking the end and that the third man in be assigned the nearest lineman to the ball. The other kickoff men could be assigned men to block depending on their position. The idea is to block off all men near where the kick lands so that your recovery man will have no trouble getting the ball. Perhaps you can suggest this idea to your coach after you show him that you can kick a ball with accuracy of direction and bounce.

Some coaches use three men on the kickoff as potential kickers. You may

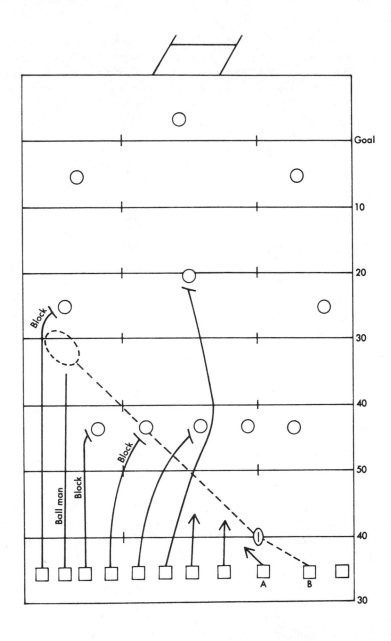

The recovery kick formation with blocking. Kickers A and B line up as though either will kick. A target on the opposite side line of B is previously selected, and on signal B runs at ball and kicks. The ball should fall in front of the man who is being blocked from the play. Kicker A delays a little and then runs by the hash mark. Kicker B must kick the ball and then fall back to prevent the roll from taking the ball out of bounds.

want to practice this play, too. If you were kicking from the center of the field, there would be more reason to use three men. The center man runs straight at the ball to be kicked, and one man on each side runs as though he were going to kick the ball to one corner of the field. The two men who will not kick veer away from the ball and allow the real kicker to make the kick. This kickoff can be most confusing to a receiving team, but I prefer the right-hash-mark kick with two men.

If your coach decides that he wants to kick downfield, then you have a choice of kicking down to a corner where the good halfback is but also where he can be bottled up in that corner. If you kick across the field, your own players have a longer time to cover the kick because the ball on a diagonal course travels farther than a ball kicked straight downfield. Plays like the foregoing ones offer you much flexibility in planning your kickoff. Here in these diagrams are some of the possibilities.

This would not be a complete book on kicking if I didn't tell you about some of the crazy kicks that have been used. When teams have not had good kickers, they have tried laying the ball on its belly and kicking it. If the kicker has his left foot near the end and kicks it in the middle with his right foot, this ball will rise above the heads of the linemen and land somewhere around the 30-yard line.

There is usually not much of a runback, because the ball hits the ground and bounces around crazily. But sometimes there is a long runback when, by chance, the ball lands right in the hands of a fast back.

Another odd kick: The ball can be kicked with the toe hitting the end. Such a kick behaves in a way that cannot be predicted.

There can be no dependence on either of these kicks for distance or direction. Any variation of the placement of the kicking foot may produce a slice out of bounds. Or the ball may go a few yards. Practice these kicks only for fun to see how crazily a football can behave.

Most kickoffs that are run back for touchdowns are high kicks down the middle. The kickoff return play may vary from a straight blocking down the middle to variations in which a plan is set up to start up the middle and then plan the blocking to create a path up one sideline. The sideline plan is usually the more successful.

Another variation of the kickoff is to send a ball down the middle with a low-trajectory place kick that will land around the 30-yard line and then roll. By rolling the ball between two potential receivers, you always have the possibility that each one may go for it or that neither one may do so. This is a free-ball situation, and I have seen a man on the kicking team recover this ball for a touchdown. Yet I am sure that every coach has told his players many times always to get possession of the ball on the kickoff. Never forget, however, that it is always a free ball on the kickoff after it has gone 10 yards.

The Kickoff and the Recovery Kick (The On-Side Kick)

After you have learned to drop-kick, you'll find that you have a great advantage on the kickoff. You can stand there on that hash mark until the moment you decide to kick, and no one can know where you are going to kick. You can look over the alignment of your opponents and then kick to the poorest runner or deliver the recovery kick.

Keep practicing the fundamentals. Make use of the balance you have achieved; aim your left foot; hold the ball in two hands down in front of your kicking foot. Kick, follow-through, and put your kicking foot down. Then step back if you want to kill the roll, or keep walking if you want to speed it up. It's a lot of fun to stand there on the kickoff looking over at your opponents and then deciding what you will do to confuse them.

As your coach will probably tell you, the kicker is usually expected to be the safety man for his team on the kickoff. When you kick, you plant your left foot and kick the ball. Then you wait to see what develops. If your team gets down fast and there is no runback, you'll not be needed. But if some fast receiving back outwits and outruns your teammates, then you are the last one to make the tackle to save the touchdown. As a kicker you have lots of responsibilities for the success of the team play on the kickoff. It is a little different on a punt, where you expect the No. 2 back on your punting team to be the safety man looking for the runback.

If your coach wants to try the cross-field recovery kick, plan to line up a target for the spot you will kick toward. Do this before the game begins when you are looking for other targets on the field. Work during the week with the player who will be assigned to be the recovery man, and let him know what target you aim for. On the day of the game tell him again. This information will help to make sure of the success of your recovery kick.

Learning to be a kicker is a matter of mind and muscle.

8

The Inner Game of Kicking the Football

Learning to be a football kicker is a matter of mind and muscle. A kicker is made up of an intricate musculature and all of this is governed by complex mental controls. Our brain is like a computer. It is a most sophisticated one. An expert on computers has said that if we were to build a computer as complicated as our brain, it would take ten billion electronic cells. The casing to house it would have to be larger than the Empire State building. It has also been said that this might be possible in the years to come but who would operate such a computer? Of course, each of us has the computer and the operator capability now. Do you have any idea of the great possibilities within reach of our brains?

We marvel at the new multiple war heads on missiles and their ability to home-in on a target. Miraculously our own brain can do even more wonderful things in controlling thoughts and actions. A defensive safety man can watch the trajectory of a high spiral punt and put himself in position to catch it, while also planning to avoid possible tacklers as he prepares to catch the ball and make his way up the field. He had to compute the point of "interception" depending upon his observed speed of the ball, wind speed, and the rate of increase of velocity as the ball came down. How is this done? He does it by feeding into his computer data from all of his senses. His computer takes this information and then compares it with stored data (memories of other successes and failures in catching footballs.)

These computations are made in a flash. Orders are issued to the muscles of the arms, legs and all other muscles involved in catching, running and stopping. Then, he "just runs". All of these computations and the decisions are made instantly. This is the subconscious activity in which there is no thinking about what to do, just doing.

This procedure is called skill automation, which is also the aim of kicking the football—to be able to just do it. We want you to learn all of the fundamentals which are involved in kicking the football and then be able to

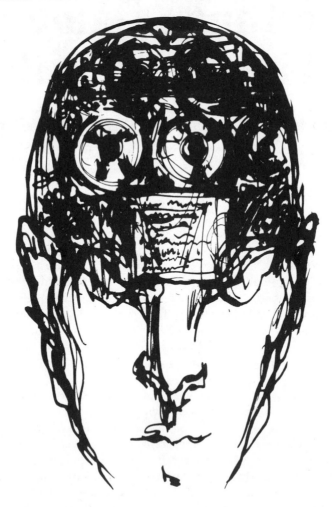

The brain is like a computer.

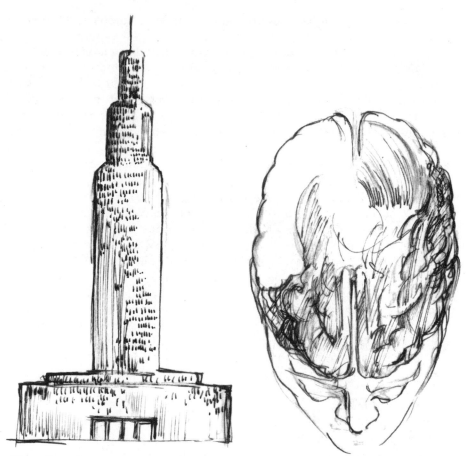

The casing to house a computer as complicated as your brain would have to be larger than the Empire State building.

kick it without thinking. In your subconscious, you will know that your body will be balanced, your eyes will be on the ball, the ball will be in the right place on your foot, and that your foot will come through the swing with a powerful whip with a fine follow-through.

You will spend many hours performing repetitions of the fundamentals of kicking the football to program your computer, starting with the beginning drills in which you kick the ball without taking steps and finally kicking with full steps. It takes at least one thousand of these repetitions to know what this skill is all about. Gradually as these repetitions proceed you will not have to think each time about the placement of the ball on your foot, or swinging your leg straight through without it crossing over. When these basics are established and programmed in your computer, you'll just kick.

Can you remember the early days of learning to ride a bicycle? You fell over and then the next time you learned to turn the handle bars for balance. Some days you thought that you would never get the "hang of it" but you eventually did. It became automatic. You no longer had to think about turning the handle bars for balance, your computer directed the turning. You just did it. This is what happens in the kicking of a football after a thousand kicks. Your computer gets programmed. Your skill becomes automatic. We can say that you kick with your subconscious and you wipe out thinking about it each time you kick. To accomplish this takes the development of mental skills and thousands of kicks.

Many people use the words conscious and subconscious as common words, as though they were simple words and ideas to understand. They also use such words as "psyched up", "all hopped up", "being ready", etc. Coaches attribute great performances of individuals and teams to such reasons without really knowing the implications.

We have coaches tell us, "I cannot get my team psyched up for the game." Many coaches in the past, and we suppose will in the future, say that an athlete's performance is 90% psychological. We doubt if any of these coaches knew what was involved in the procedure of getting "psyched up" or making use of the power of the brain to get better performances. Yet, we know from the research of scientists and the observations of psychologists that there are ways of improving performance through psychological means.

Let's look at these words conscious and subconscious. One writer has substituted the names of Self I and Self II. Perhaps this is easier to understand than conscious and subconscious. What is Self I? It is that part of your mind which seems to be located on the left side of your brain for right handed people. Here all learning begins from simple walking to the understanding of language. Additionally, all of our nerves send their messages there so that we may make decisions. Finally, we also get the full effect of our feelings and seem to translate them into what is called stress. It is generally believed that memory is based in this area of the brain but later transferred to the subconcious or Self II, where the habits of muscular control are built.

When you first learn to roller skate, ride a bicycle, throw a ball or drive an automobile, it is the conscious or Self I that is absorbed in the activity of deciding which hand or foot will do what. After a period of learning, Self II or the subconscious seems to take over and directs the muscles in their action without conscious thinking. These actions are called automatic. This is what we achieve for the kicker—the ability to just kick the ball without thinking of balance, position of the ball on the foot, any possibility of fail-

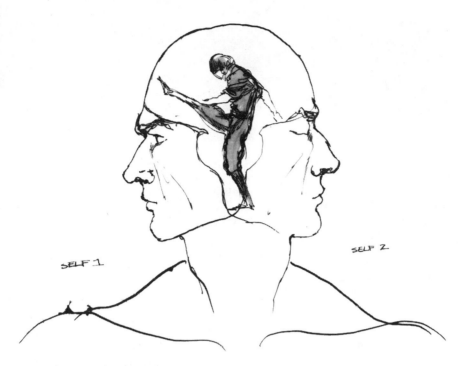

The transferal of the movements to 'self 2' from 'self 1'.

ing, his follow-through, or whether the ball will come to him straight from center or go over his head. It seems as though there are a hundred ideas that can go through the kicker's mind, if he wants them to. If they do, his kick will not be the best. This thinking during the time the ball is kicked must be eliminated. When you can do this, your kicks will leave the foot in perfect form and with maximum impetus because your Self II has taken over. Folks will say that you kick automatically.

How do we learn to let Self II take control? In the act of kicking the football, there are two most important things for the kicker to know: (1) what part of the football you want your foot to contact and (2) what place on your foot you want to contact the football. To punt the football, start with the ball in the palm of your right hand, if you are a right footed kicker, and place it on your foot. Note that I do not say DROP. Drop does not mean accurate placement, which is what we want. Draw a line and chalk it from the base of your big toe, on your foot, to a point which is the midpoint of the outside line of your shoe. For the ideal punt, you want the bottom seam of the ball to land on the center of gravity of your foot, where there is rigid bone. When this position of ball and ankle coincide, a great kick results.

**Draw a line from the base of
the big toe to the outside
of the shoe.**

When you are able to achieve this position of the ball on your ankle, remember how it FEELS, and for future kicks try to achieve this same feel. Associate this feel with your good stance and the ease of the ball leaving your foot. When it feels good, it is a good kick.

We have found that by using a blindfold we can accentuate this awareness of the feel of the football on the foot correctly. You can do it yourself. What you do is attach the blindfold with open eyes, pick your target, then pull the blindfold down and kick. Before you lift the blindfold decide where the ball is. Then, take off the blindfold and compare reality with your judgement. After many trials and successes, you will find that you get better placement of the ball on your foot and that you become more aware of the feel of it leaving your foot. Your accuracy will improve with practice.

Great kickers know where their foot is by the feel. They also know where it is in space without looking at it. By using the blindfold practice, you will too. Feeling will tell you what you want to know about the kick. Listening to the sound of the impact will tell you much about your kick. These feelings help to get Self II in control of the action.

It seems quite normal for us in sports to want to know about the performance. Was it good or was it bad? What was my score? This is the first judgement that Self I makes. However, for the best performance, we have to concern ourselves with the next kick and how the foot contacts the ball. If you feel the kick was not right, then forget it and move to the next one. A kick that felt good can be repeated. With repetition, it is going to be part of

By using a blindfold and practicing kicking, you can accentuate your awareness of the feel of the football.

the important information in the subconscious that will make good kicks possible in the future. For this habit formation to become an integral part of Self II's action, it is necessary to stop evaluating and just keep kicking. This is why I recommend kicking for distance be limited to once each week.

When you can accept the fact that kicking a football depends upon the mental as well as the physical, you are on your way to better performance. This is what we are discussing. Let's see what we do specifically to improve your performance.

Today we know that visualization and imagery are as important in learning and the production of the skill as is the physical kicking of the football. Visualization is a way of rehearsing in your imagination exactly what you will do in the physical practice skill. It is the way you program Self II to read out to the muscles when you want to kick. Let's try it. Sit in a chair, close your eyes, and go through all of the movements of kicking a football in your imagination. Imagine that you have the ball in your hands, feel the seams and go through the details of placing it on your foot and kicking it.

Now, let's try the game situation in which you will be involved one of these days. Take a couple of deep breaths, relax and let your mind take over. The coach says, "Go in and kick," you step in the huddle, you get the snap signal, you look downfield at the target to kick at, you go back to your position and stand relaxed, you look for the ball, you focus on the ball and watch its revolutions as it comes back to you, because you are punting you gather it in to your hip, you step with your right foot, and, when the left lands, you place the ball on your foot and kick it. It felt good. It was a good kick. You knew it was going to be a good kick. It went out on the 2 yard line. You hear the roar of the crowd. Then, you open your eyes. You have rehearsed a perfect kick, mentally. Some day this event will take place just as you have practiced it with your eyes open on a real field and in a real game. You'll be great because you have done it all before in your visualization practice. Keep it up.

When you are on the field, you can go through this visualization process in less than a second. Twenty five seconds is allowed to pass before the whistle for "too much time" blows. So, you have time to do it in the huddle or immediately thereafter. When you do this, your subconscious believes that you have actually kicked the football and takes over for a second kick. Now, it will be automatic.

This visualization, imagery and rehearsal are not new ideas in Europe. The East Germans and the Russians have done a great deal with these mental practices for some years. We were exposed to these ideas back in 1932. The first and only book on the subject appeared here in 1959.

These techniques have been most helpful to gymnasts, divers and recently for our ski team in the Winter Olympics at Lake Placid. Some athletes have demonstrated amazing improvements in their performances after making use of this visualization. Don't expect immediate improvement. It takes many rehearsals to place this information in the subconscious.

A fine time for visualization is when you are ready for sleep. Lay back relaxed and with closed eyes, go through the details of the kick. If you go to sleep, fine. If not, repeat and repeat.

Most relaxation techniques are tied up with the ideas of heaviness or warmth. Progressively this works out with arms, legs and then body. One way to accomplish this is to use this method: (1) Lie down and take two breaths; (2) close your eyes and feel the right arm getting heavy; (3) think heaviness in your left arm, heavy, heavy; (4) now feel heaviness in the legs; (5) feel heaviness just under the "belly button"; (6) return to the arms and feel them getting warm; (7) repeat with the other arms and legs; (8) feel the warmth in your "belly button area"; (9) feel your cool forehead.

The first time you try this, you may not have great success but do not stop. It will happen if you repeat it. It takes practice like all other mental techniques. These exercises can be practiced either sitting up or lying down. You'll find after awhile that you can completely relax in a minute. In the beginning it will take somewhat longer.

When you are waiting on the sidelines to go in and kick, do these relaxation exercises. When your coach says, "relax", you'll know what to do. Go through these exercises. When you feel that you have to do something else, here is an idea for you, too. Sit down and feel your breathing. Become aware of every intake and exhale. Feel your diaphragm moving up and down inside you body like a piston. We will guarantee that you'll have no difficulty with tension when you go in to kick if you'll follow this advice and programming for your pre-kick time. You'll go in and do the job **without thinking**.

In order to be a successful kicker, you should posses a high level of overall fitness.

9
Successful Kickers Are Accomplished Athletes

In Order to be a successful kicker, you should be well developed. There are many aspects of strength; many factors are behind the long kick. There is determination, training, heredity, nutrition, nerves, character, heart, brain, and muscles.

You have approximately 500 voluntary muscles in your body under the direct control of your will. About 250 of these are involved with your kicking. Only 50 of these are in your leg. In other words, your kicking uses some 200 voluntary muscles in the central part of your body, your neck, trunk, and head. Some of these are very small, and some are very large. They have many different shapes, and they all have special purposes.

Some of the muscles that are most important are *not* under direct control of your will. These work automatically while you sleep and while you are awake. You seldom consider them, yet their care is more important than the care of the muscles in the rest of your body.

Consider, for instance, your abdominal-wall muscles. You may have the strongest legs in the world, but if your abdominal muscles are weak, you cannot be a good runner, jumper, or kicker. If your abdomen is soft and flabby, any effort makes it bulge weakly. Your arms and legs will have no reliable substance behind their action, and there is no power. Perhaps the most important muscles you have are your abdominal muscles. Remember the name *rectus abdominus*. It holds your abdomen in and contracts in sit-ups. Your abdominal muscles are far more important than the biceps, even though most men show their biceps as evidence of their strength and physical fitness.

You want to be a topnotch kicker. Work on your most important muscles; develop a foundation, or you get nowhere. Every jump, throw, or kick you make is three-quarters the work of trunk muscles. The man who is strong in the trunk will outrun or outkick his competitors. This is one of the secrets of success in athletics.

Great coaches know this fundamental and spend much time developing the trunks of their players during preseason workouts. You can be your own coach in this and many other matters. When it comes down to an analysis of whether you succeed or not, it is up to you. You are the one primarily responsible for your success or failure.

Here is a simple exercise that you can practice on for many years. It has always been called the suspension hang or the strength exercise. It is also considered a fitness test. Sit in a chair that has solid arms, or using two chairs placed shoulder width apart, grip the backs of both chairs. Hold your arms straight and bring your legs up straight in front of you. This is the L.

The "L" position for strengthening exercises.

Keep your feet steady, and keep them far out. Point your toes. How long can you hold this position? One second is something. Ten seconds is fabulous. Test your friends, and see how good they are at the L. Practice this muscle builder every day. and check your improvement on the clock.

Other isometric exercises that I recommend are the back press, the false seat, the reverse arch, and the leg push. Ask your coach about these in physical-education class.

He may want you to get into some weight training, too. This is fine for strengthening muscles, but mix it up with running and your kicking practice. Weight lifting has a tendency to build big strong muscles, but sometimes it also slows up the action of these muscles. Remember, speed is the most important asset in kicking.

In every athletic effort the abdominal muscles play an essential part. The high jump, the kicks in football, and practically every movement in baseball use these abdominal muscles. They are always in the middle of things. Not many people know this fundamental, but now you do. Never forget that strong arms and strong legs are futile unless you have a strong abdominal base to work from. Your abdominal muscles can be the secrets of your strength development and indirectly of your kicking success.

When you kick, some muscles contract, others steady the action, and a few relax. The abdominal muscles are particularly essential. The *rectus abdominus* is involved in sit-ups, so sit-ups are a phase of your physical-fitness program to take advantage of every day.

The *quadriceps extensor* muscles straighten out your leg. They are the big muscles that form the front part of your thigh. They also straighten the knee when you stand up straight from a squatting position. Try this: Stand straight, put your hands on your thighs, and sink slowly until you sit on your heels like a baseball catcher behind the plate. Feel the muscles harden. These muscles have put the upper leg in a pre-stretch condition; the quadriceps are stretched, ready for action. The action is to straighten the leg. This motion is very important in kicking the football because it provides the whip necessary to increase the speed of the foot.

The Russians have developed a set of exercises based on this principle of pre-stretch called Plyometrics. These exercises, we believe, are very important for kickers and should take the place of most weight lifting for the lower leg. They include what are called Power Bounds. These are achieved by starting from a position of a standing broad jump. In this exercise, the athlete tries to achieve height and distance in his jump from both feet. These bounds should be done continuously with no stop between them. When you first do them, you should not attempt more than about 15 yards. They are strenuous and will result in sore legs the next day. They should be repeated every other day. After a week of doing the 15 yards, you can try the next 20 yards. Do that for a week and then add another 5 yards. By this method,

The trunk muscles.

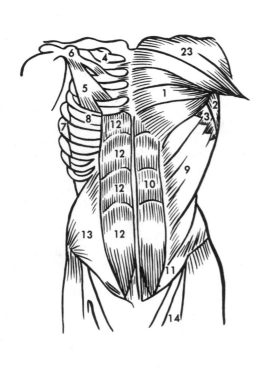
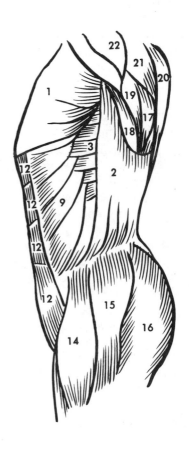

1. **Pectoralis major (Sternal fibers)**
2. **Latissimus dorsi**
3. **Serratus major anticus**
4. **Subclavius muscle**
5. **Pectoralis minor**
6. **Coraco process of the scapula**
7. **Serratus major anticus after removal of the obliquus externus abdominis**
8. **External intercostal muscle of the fifth inercostal space**
9. **External oblique of the abdomen**
10. **Tendon of external oblique**
11. **Poupart's ligament**
12. **Rectus abdominis**
13. **Internal oblique of the abdomen**
14. **Tensor facia latae**
15. **Gluteus medius**
16. **Gluteus maximus**
17. **Infraspinatus**
18. **Teres major**
19. **Teres minor**
20. **Trapezius**
21. **Deltoid**
22. **Triceps**
23. **Pectoral major (clavicular fibers)**

The thigh muscles

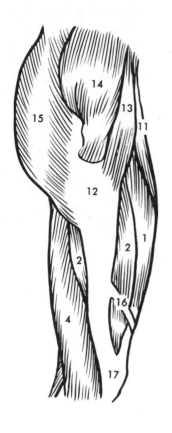 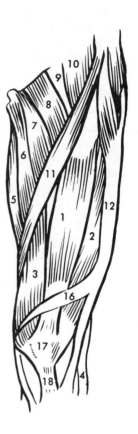

1. Rectus femoris
2. Vastus externus
3. Vastus internus
4. Biceps of leg
5. Gracilis
6. Adductor magnus
7. Adductor longus
8. Pectineus
9. Psoas

10. Iliacus
11. Sartorius
12. Ilio-tibial band
13. Tensor fasciae femoris
14. Gluteus medius
15. Gluteus maximus
16. Richer's ligament
17. Patella
18. Patella ligament

* The quadricepts extensor of the leg includes the vastus externus, vastus internus, rectus, and a deep muscle, the crureus.

over a period of two or three months, you should be able to do the whole football field.

In between the Power Bounds, you should try the one leg hops. At first try a distance of about 30 yards. Hop up on the left leg and hop back with the right leg. Do these on alternate days also.

Another great exercise to improve balance and to develop leg power is a Russian exercise that comes from the dancing. This is a deep knee bend on one foot; you extend your kicking leg out forward as you go down on your balance leg. It is easy to go down but hard to keep your balance (put your hands forward). It is even harder to come up again and not stagger. It is also easier to do this maneuver quickly than slowly. When you can do a deep knee bend on either foot down and up while keeping your balance, you are good.

Next try the Russian kick step. Go down on one leg with the other forward and not touching the ground, keeping yours arms folded. Change feet. Change again and again. This is a typical Cossack step. When you can do it six or seven times, jump to your feet and yell.

There is much more to the kicking of the football than the strength of the quadriceps muscles and the full squat with variations. For example, the left knee is never bent while kicking with the right foot, but this kind of kicking

The Cossack step exercise.

is great training. The mastery of the high kick (follow-through) is vital. You must train yourself, muscles and brain. Remember that the left arm helps the right foot get a full follow-through. So arm strength is important, too.

In the fall of 1968, I attended the Olympic Games in Mexico and saw the best athletes in the world. I saw them in Rome and in Berlin, too. These men make doing things look very easy, and we say they have a secret. That secret is skill developed over a long period of time. It is no miracle how they developed it.

You can go a long way, perhaps all the way, toward building comparable skill. Some athletes develop easily, and some get their skill the hard way. Others never make it. If you really want to be a great kicker and football player, think about the suggestions given here and make them a part of your daily living.

Skill is largely the product of your nervous system. It is inside you. How does it develop? First, the eyes, ears, nose, skin, and tissues of your body pick up information and send it to your brain. It tells you what is going on outside so that you can do something about it.

In athletics the eye is of great importance, as everyone knows. But what not everyone knows is that athletic skill depends fundamentally on the incoming sensations from your arms and legs and other parts of your body. When you kick a ball, you cannot look at your feet, your arms, and where the ball will go. You must keep your eye on the ball and let your skill do the job for you.

The look you take before you get ready to kick is to aim yourself and the ball. When you take the ball in your hands, all you can do is to feel where your arms and legs are and what you are doing with them. Today it is possible to see yourself on movies or video tape. This help can be of inestimable value to you. If it is available, make full use of it.

Do you think you know accurately where your hands and feet are when you can't see them? Try this test. Stand with your arms wide apart and close your eyes. Now bring your right index finger up to the top of your nose in one swift swoop and watch out for your eye! Now try the left one. Can you improve with practice? Certainly, and that is the way to develop skill.

Try to put your finger in your opposite ear with your eyes closed. Do it more quickly. Your success in this test depends entirely on the sensations coming from your muscles, joints, and skin and on your ability to feel correctly. This feeling ability is called your kinesthetic sense. This is the sense you must develop in order to get the right hold on the ball quickly and automatically for a punt or drop-kick. It takes lots of practice, and some of this practice will pay off if it is done blindfolded.

The essence of skill is to know what you are doing by the feel of yourself. One help that you can make good use of is to close your eyes when you're about to go to sleep and try to picture in your mind each part of the skill you are trying to learn. Then follow each part through until you have completed the skill in your "mind's eye." For kicking, picture your aim, your hand under the ball, your step, your leg coming forward, placing the ball on your

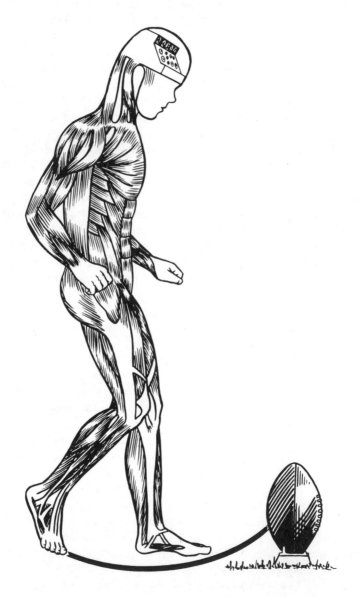

The brain is the "computer" that directs the muscles of the body to make kicking a reflex action.

foot, your foot carrying the ball, and releasing it for a punt by depressing your toe. Then see the ball traveling downfield to your target. Think it through again and again until you drop off to sleep. This is a system for setting nerve "switches" so that when you are ready to kick, your nervous system will direct your muscles to do what you want them to do. Such thinking is a very important aspect of your skill development. Balance depends on sensory nerves and the whole complex of your middle-ear semicircular canals. Certain exercises can help you with your balance. One very good one is to stand on your balance foot and pedal with your kicking foot as long as possible. Maybe you can do it 100 times. If you'll do this exercise every day, you'll develop much better balance and be able to stand on your left foot for a long period of time without having to put your kicking foot down.

To be the kind of kicker you want to be, you must develop some conditioned reflexes. A reflex is just a common act the body does for itself when the occasion arises. For example, cross your legs and hit your knee tendon just below the kneecap. If you do it right, your leg kicks. Why? Because when you hit your tendon, you stretch it and its activating muscle (front of thigh) contracts, making your knee jerk. Of what use is this reflex? When you land from a jump, this same tendon is stretched. The same muscle contracts, and you are let down easily. This reflex is very useful in athletics. Otherwise, you would land with a terrible bump.

When something is flying toward you, your tendency is to close your eyes and flinch. This is a reflex to protect you, too. Because of this reflex, however, football players must be taught to keep their eyes open when they block or tackle. Seasoned players take advantage of beginning blockers, knowing that they will close their eyes.

Reflexes increase speed. Your spinal cord, when educated, makes a quick short circuit and shortcut to action. Quickness sometimes saves even lives.

The best demonstration of a reflex is what happens when you touch your finger to a fire. Your reflex action will take your finger away almost half a second before you know about the fire.

Such reflexes are valuable assets. Practice develops conditioned reflexes. There are kicking reflexes that you'll develop by daily practice with the fundamentals.

In the quick kick, for instance, you practice putting that kicking foot back and then placing your balance foot behind it. After a while you will do this without thinking when the signal is given in the huddle. You have learned it. It will become habitual and subconscious. Your nervous system will know it, and you can devote attention to other things. Your quick-kick steps will become a reflex act. Your body has learned the complex movements of walking, running, balancing, and now you can make it learn the skills of kicking a football where you want it and how you want it to go there.

10
Kicking Is A Joint Effort

Up to now you have been concentrating on the hows of kicking the football, but it may help you to know a little about some of the whys. You have been kicking the football by means of the combined effect of your foot and many joints. Your balance depends on joints and a foot. The ball is propelled by the ankle joint. To keep on kicking, you must take good care of your feet and all the joints that make up your feet, legs, and hips. Your shoes and their condition are very important to you. Your feet are your wheels for movement and for the ball's propulsion.

Watch a football player in action and you see a powerhouse of activity. All his faculties work together so smoothly that they are not aware of individual units. There is great teamwork of muscles and joints.

The most obvious and yet the most unthought-of thing about a boy or man running, jumping, or kicking is that he is working many joints: knees, neck, back, hip, and ankles. Think what would happen to you if you had no joints. You can't run with even one joint immobilized, say, the right knee. Do you remember the character in a popular TV Western who had a stiff knee? He couldn't run or kick, of course. We have some very important joints used in kicking, and the principal one is the ankle.

If you'd like to get an inside look at how an ankle really works, go down to the butcher store and buy a beef hock. It costs little and will reveal many interesting facts to you when you take it apart. You could learn which parts are muscle, which are cartilage, and which are ligaments.

Your body has many kinds of joints. They are known by such names as hinge, pivot, saddle, ball-and-socket, gliding, and several others with long Latin names. The ones that you'll be most interested in are those concerned with your balance foot and your kicking leg. Just any joint consists of bones, cartilages, synovial membrane, ligaments, tendons, muscles with nerve connections, and blood for nourishment. The ankle joint has all these components and works first as a saddle joint.

If you decided to take the cow's ankle (beef hock) apart, here's what you'll find that is similar to and also what is different from your own ankle joint.

Look for the Achilles' tendon. This tendon is the attachment of the large muscles (calf in men and round steak in cow). It pulls the heel and extends the foot and toe. It is in the back of the ankle and is sometimes called the heel muscle by people who do not know anatomy. This tendon makes it possible for you to move the front part of your foot up and down. It enables you to depress your toe and release the football for your punt. Any problem with this tendon affects your punting.

The cow's hind foot is long and thin. She walks on two toenails with her heel in the air. The horse walks on one toenail; the elephant on five, as we do. Your forward push when walking or running should use all five toes. That is why we have them. Do you use them all?

If you decide to go ahead with the further dissecting of this hock, cut off the meat (muscle) attached to the Achilles' tendon. Pull on this tendon and see the joint move. Follow the Achilles' tendon down to the heel. Find other tendons. Follow them around the joint, and see how they protect this joint and hold it together. Pull on them, and see how they move the joint.

Locate your own Achilles' tendon and the two prominent bones on the sides of the ankle. The outside bony prominence is the end of the fibula bone (the one that is usually broken in a skiing accident. Can you figure out why?). The inside prominence is the end of the tibia. These two prominences grasp and protect the astragalus on which the hinge joint works underneath. You can hardly feel the other bones of the ankle and foot in front. These are tied fairly tight with collars of ligaments, allowing little motion.

The chief business of the ankle is to flex and extend, as in rising on the toes. The ankle is kept steady by: (1) the ends of the bones; (2) the lateral ligaments; and (3) the tendons. The sideway and rotary movements of the foot are largely accomplished in the several joints below the ankle. One fine exercise for strengthening these muscles is a toe rise with weights.

Around the ankle are the internal and external lateral ligaments. These are the ankle ligaments that are most commonly strained or sprained. Strains or sprains happen when you turn your ankle because of carelessness, untrained feet, rough ground, rolling stones, or putting your foot down when you haven't felt or seen where it is to go.

Depending on what is injured, ankle injuries are either fractures, dislocations, strains, or sprains. Take a look at the illustration included here for an idea of what can happen and how important it is for you to exercise your ankle in order to prevent some of these things from happening to you. A bad sprain will limit your kicking career and it may even end it.

Any damage to your ankle, even if it is only a strain, will affect your kicking. I would always advise that you see a doctor when there is an ankle injury.

A sprained ankle with torn ligaments and displacement is bad business. It hurts, disables, and takes as much time to cure as a broken bone, up to six weeks. Every case is different, requiring professional judgment, and that is why I recommend seeing a doctor.

If you have an ankle injury, get out of the game. There should be some ice to keep down the swelling. If the ankle hurts, don't walk on it until you have seen a doctor and he tells you to do so.

You need to develop strong ankles, educated ankles, well-managed ankles, accustomed to adjusting themselves automatically to rough footing and sudden stresses.

Hiking over rough country makes tough ankles and legs. A rough climbing mile will give your feet a thousand variations to meet. Flat sidewalks and smooth roads don't do it. Some football teams have part of their training on the beach. Here every step is an adjustment for joints. This training is very good. Running in sand takes more effort than running on a smooth field. Educate your feet to handle the ground so that they will not be caught unawares when you hit unusuall conditions on the field.

You educate your whole body and brain at the same time, for with every step you use more than 100 muscles, ligaments, joints, and nerve connections, all working together, coordinated, another evidence of the great teamwork of your body.

One of the best exercise situations I know of is to work out a travel routine for yourself consisting of a line of pieces of wood or flat pieces of stone. Underneath them place some rollers that make stepping on them difficult. Try running through this group of stones and pieces of wood.

Do it slowly at first, and adjust to the rolling of the pieces of wood. Speed it up, and keep some kind of record to see how much you can improve your time. Maybe you can mix in a couple of tires just to make the course more difficult. As the days go by, you will develop stronger and more adjustable muscles, ligaments, and joints.

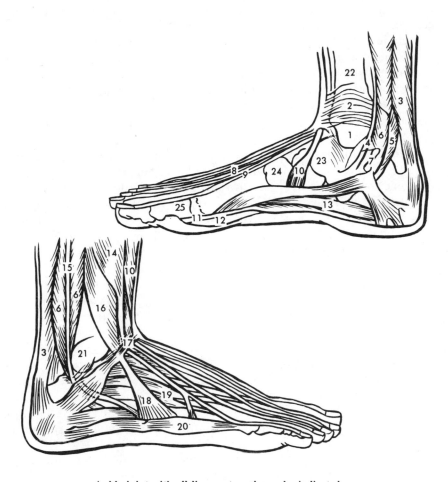

Ankle joint with all ligaments and muscles indicated.

1. Tibia malleolus (ankle)
2. Internal annular ligament
3. Tendon Achillis
4. Tibialis posticus (posterior)
5. Long flexor or great toe
6. Peroneus brevis
7. Flexor longus digitorumpectis
8. Long extensor of toes
9. Extensor of great toe
10. Tibialis anticus
11. Long flexor of great toe
12. Flexor hallucis brevis pedis
13. Abductor hallucis pedis

14. Extensor longus digitorum
15. Peroneus longus
16. Personeus tertius
17. Anterior annular ligament
18. Peroneus tertius
19. Short extensor of toes
20. Abductor miinimi pedis
21. External malleolus (fibula)
22. Tibia
23. Astragalus
24. Navicular
25. Cuneiform bones

The ankle joint of your kicking foot is your rifle for shooting the projectile that is the football. Your exercises will make it strong, durable, and capable of fine accuracy.

Included in this book is an illustration of a card that we use at clinics for examining potential kickers. You'll notice there is a question of "Balance foot toe position." The evaluations are 1, 2, 3. If you walk with toes straight ahead, somewhat like Indians, your rating would be a number 1. And 3 means that you walk with toes pointing out. Number 2 is highly desirable, because such a position makes it easier to aim and balance yourself.

A number 3 rating may mean weak arches, and it surely indicates a need for a lot of foot exercise. If you think you are a number 3, ask your doctor for some exercise ideas. He may also suggest some wedging of your shoes to give the long arch an easier effort in carrying your body around. Wiggling your toes inside your shoes is a very good exercise and one that you can do even while sitting. Squinch your toes in your shoes. Repeat it fifty times each time you think of it. In this way you can pile up several hundred per day and strengthen your muscles.

Indians walk and run with actually a slight turn-in of their feet. This is a good pattern. Work on it and you'll have no trouble with your balance foot in its position or your kicking foot when it contacts the ball for your shortest or longest kick.

Have you ever taken the national physical education tests? Your physical education teacher must have these tests. If you haven't done so, ask him for the chance to take them. If you qualify, he can recommend you for the honor emblems issued by the American Association of Health, Physical Education and Recreation, which is a part of the National Education Association. These tests consist of push-ups, sit-ups, pull-ups, some running, and certain skill tests.

Have you ever had an opportunity to try your grip and see how many pounds you can grip? The nearer you can grip the number of pounds you weigh, the better physical condition you are in.

How far can you run in ten minutes? This is a good test of your physical condition, too. You should be able to do a mile or better. Your kicking depends on your overall physical condition.

Take another good look at the sketch of the right foot with its bony framework, ligaments, and muscles. You'll notice that the big toe is connected to the ankle by three bones called metatarsals and phalanges. The seven bones that make up the arch of the ankle are called tarsals.

We say that we punt with the first metatarsal because it is the bone that connects the big toe to the ankle. The football fits on top of the bones and lies across the ankle, sloping down in back so that when the toe is depressed, a nice smooth punt will result.

If you haven't already done so, try what was recommended in an earlier chapter: Take off your shoe and sock of your kicking foot. Draw a line with a Magic Marker from the base of the big toe to the midpoint of the outside of your foot. This line is called the metatarsal line. That is the line that the seam of the football should lie on for a perfect left-spiral punt.

For punting you need a shoe that fits tightly and has a soft toe. Otherwise, the ball will not roll off your foot smoothly when your toe is depressed. A wool sock dangling over your shoe takes away from the propelling power. Buy a shoe that fits as tightly as possible over a thin sock, rather than a loose shoe and heavy wool sock. I have just designed a shoe with no laces and a zipper on the side. It will be ideal for punting unless some restrictions are put into the football rules. I suggest high shoes rather than low shoes. You'll understand their advantage when you look at the ankle.

For the place kick or drop kick, a hard-toed shoe is necessary. An extension of the sole with a concave cut will produce fabulous results. The professionals have rules against it. Maybe the federation and college rulemakers will do likewise another year, but today it is legal. The square toe has an advantage over the round toe. Here again, the shoe should fit snugly, and there should be no sock hanging over and no shoelaces tied in front. Be sure your toenails are cut square across to prevent ingrowing toenails. Your foot is your rifle and must always be in the best condition.

Choose a Ball Sized for You

In earlier days, football players of all ages and sizes were forced to use man-size footballs. This limitation is no longer necessary, because I designed footballs for players of various ages way back in 1932. We made a study of the foot sizes and hand sizes of boys in relation to grown-ups and came up with a football size for elementary schools and one for the junior high school age.

If you are in elementary school under eleven years of age, you should be kicking and passing the ball that has the following dimensions: circumference (long axis) 25½ to 25¾ inches; long axis 10 inches; circumference (short axis) 18½ inches to 18¾ inches; and short axis 5¾ inches. This ball is called the junior football.

For boys in junior high, we have designed a football with the following dimensions: circumference (long axis) at least 26¼ inches but not more than 26½ inches; long axis 10¾ inches; circumference (short axis) 19¼ inches; and short axis 6¼ inches. This is the sub-senior ball.

We find that these balls fit the feet and shoes of most boys in our schools and help them develop their kicking ability as they grow. With a football made to fit your feet and your hands, you'll find it much easier to develop the skills this book talks about.

11
What It Takes
to be a Great Kicker

You have decided to be the kicker for your football team. You will be successful because you have made a personal commitment to learn how to kick a football to the best of your God-given capabilities. To succeed is one of life's greatest aims. First, it is necessary to have a clear picture of the best way to do things before being able to do them successfully. Visualize yourself winning and succeeding by the action of **your** foot.

Reading this book indicates that you are serious about becoming a better kicker. But reading is not the whole answer. A lot of hard work must be done in order to achieve success. Work will become your food, your breath, your entertainment, and your life. Keep in mind that the only place the word "success" comes before the word "work" is in the dictionary.

You must have a goal, a specific objective. Aim high. Each skill that you master is a step toward that goal. While almost all athletes have lofty goals early in their lives, some individuals are deterred from their goals as the road to success becomes more difficult. The price that an athlete must pay to do the job well makes the word "athlete" almost sacred. A dedicated athlete should absorb as much coaching, learning, and information as possible about the skill involved in his sport. His motto should be "What I give I will always have, but what I keep is lost forever." Life is what you want to make of it. Life's greatest victory is over self. Your goal should be to become such a fine kicker that everyone wants you on their team. You will not have "to make" the team. They will come seeking you.

You must have *desire*. When you know what your goal is, you must work toward it avidly. This means having a burning desire to excel, to be a winner. It means that you hate mediocrity. You hustle and show enthusiasm, thereby making difficult tasks and sacrifices easier.

You must have *pride* in your team and in your own achievement. You must be proud of what you are doing, proud of being an athlete, proud of being your team's kicker. It takes a certain amount of pride to do anything well.

You must have *courage*: the courage to try and the courage to overcome obstacles, handicaps, failures, and defeats. This is real courage. It takes courage to stand in your kicking spot in punt formation 12 yards away from your protecting line while seven or eight linemen rush at you. You have to keep your eye on the ball. If you are not a great big fellow, it takes a little more courage to perform this skill. With lots of practice in the fundamentals of kicking, you'll have little trouble when this situation happens. The practicing you do during the off-season months will be a good indication of how much you want to succeed.

It takes *determination* to be a great player. How badly do you want to make your school team? How badly do you want to be the best kicker on your squad? When you are determined to reach your goal, you keep trying, you stick it out when the going is toughest. When you have this kind of determination, you accept criticism, and *you don't quit*. It's a great mistake to think that you can learn to be a great kicker in a short time. Maybe you'll have to work hard for months to acquire the skill you want. Maybe you'll want to go back and check up on your skill in the early pages of this book. When you are in competition, other players are going to make things tough for you. You must be ready for them, physically and mentally. It will not be all glory; there'll be heavy going and some disappointments. There'll be lots of labor ahead, and only with the determination will you make it.

It takes *confidence* in yourself, your coach, and your teammates to succeed. You must be realistic; you must be honest with yourself. You gain confidence when you know you have paid the price in extra effort and sacrifices. Follow the motto of the Air Force: "The difficult we do immediately. The impossible takes a little longer." With confidence in yourself you can attain your highest potential as a football player and kicker.

It is going to take *sacrifices* to make you and your team succeed. The greater the athlete, usually the greater the sacrifices he has made in achieving his goal. Sacrifices are of two kinds: (1) giving up something for your personal good or the good of the team, and (2) doing something extra for the team. To be a winner in athletics, you must accept and abide by a code of training rules. This means that you cannot do many things that nonathletes do. When you put forth extra effort during the off-season, you become stronger, quicker, faster, and more skillful than your competition. This is that something extra for you and your team. When you make sacrifices, you have the right mental attitude. Mental attitude is often the critical difference between two great teams that meet. Your mental attitude will help determine the team attitude when the football season rolls around.

It takes *dedication*, hard work, and extra effort to be a great player. This is the real secret of championship performance. Great athletes practice extra. Great athletes do extra things for the team, the coach, and the school. Doing only what you are told is not enough. For excellence, you must give out extra effort during the off-season and in season. Perhaps the highest compliment that can be paid an athlete is to say that he is dedicated.

It takes *discipline* to be your best. It isn't what you have or even what you do that expresses your worth as a man, but what you are. It takes a certain toughness not to let others sway you away from what you feel is right. When you discipline yourself, you prove yourself a man. This is what we mean when we say you are mentally tough. You help develop mental toughness when you do something every day in your development as an athlete.

It takes *patience* to be a great athlete. There is no magic, no shortcut, and very little luck to gaining success in athletics. It is not easy. If it were, there would be more great athletes, great kickers, great teams. When you pay the price in extra effort during the off-season, you'll be that much better prepared when opportunity knocks during the regular season.

Football is a great game, and you need character to play it successfully. Yours is a great heritage. We have great football players of all sizes, and they have various degrees of skill and talent. However, each truly great athlete has paid the extra price in sacrifice, hard work, and extra effort. How will you compare with the other kickers who want to make your team? Are you ready to put in that extra work to become a great kicker?

On some days you'll kick well, and on others, for no apparent reason, you won't do so well. Take it as it comes, and don't get discouraged. There'll be a wet day, and your kicks won't roll the way they did on the dry day. Take it as it comes.

How you react when things don't go your way is vital. Will you give up, or will you try harder than ever? Unfortunately, occasionally your center will literally "roll" the snap to you. Will you remember to pivot and kick the ball as well as possible - without berating your teammate for his failure to snap the ball properly? Sure you can. Just tell him, "That was a slip - it will not happen again." By the same token, every time you have a fine snap, take time to compliment the center. Whenever appropriate, tell your offensive line that they are doing a great job. Don't ever forget the value of positive reinforcement. It doesn't cost you a "cent" and the compliment means more than you'll ever know to your teammates.

One means of evaluating a kicker is by the use the of the card, a replica of which is included in the appendices. I use this card when I conduct kicking clinics. You can use the card to help determine where you'll have to make adjustments.

You may wonder about some of the factors on the card and how they affect kicking. First, you find that balance is listed. Because of the emphasis this book has given to balance, you know why it is important. There are many ways to check the working of the semicircular canals in your ears, which affects your balance. The one we like to use, however, is the walk down the sideline with the eyes closed tight.

On this test, we have found that the right-footed kicker strays to his right and the left-footed kicker to his left. This phenomenon gives you an idea why lost people tend to walk in circles, rather big circles, but circles, nevertheless.

The degree of deviation on this test will help a kicking coach to determine how much you should allow when picking a target on the field. You can do some figuring on your own. If you are off 5 yards, that is a good allowance to start with. As you practice kicking and work on your balance, you'll find that you need to allow fewer yards for deviating. You'll get to be much more accurate and better balanced.

If you are off more than 10 yards at the goal line after walking the 50 yards down the sideline with your eyes closed, perhaps some more checking should be done. I would like to know if you have ever had a concussion, a high fever that lasted a long time, or an injury to either of your legs or hips. Maybe a medical checkup is indicated.

Serious injuries can make a difference in your ability to balance and stand on one foot. You are now aware of how important it is for joints to work correctly and easily. Injuries to these parts of your body can make a lot of difference in the performance of your kicking leg. Knee injuries are especially troublesome. They may interfere with a full follow-through.

I hope that you do not smoke. Tobacco has some devious effects, and I am sure that you may have some ideas on that score without my using a lot of words. If you want to be a great kicker, don't smoke anything.

The card may make you ask what difference it makes whether you can dance or whether you have an ear for music. Those factors may be an indication of your timing. We have found that good dancers make better kickers than poor dancers. Good rope skippers tend to be good kickers, too.

Decide right now as you finish reading this book that you'll find out more about yourself in order really to "Know thyself," as Socrates put it so many centuries ago. Then make plans for improvement. Increase the number of push-ups and sit-ups that you can do, and keep an accurate record from day to day. Have a bulletin board in your room and keep score on yourself there. Then your progress will be obvious to you. Decide on your goals, and do everything you can to attain them.

When you encounter a potentially painful situation, don't run from it. Face it, and if necessary, take it as a part of the game. If you do this once, then you can add one victory to your stock of courage. Every time you overcome the instinct to flinch from danger, you'll be stronger and more courageous. Such willpower can be developed and is part of the intangible education of a great player.

Becoming an outstanding kicker is not an easy job. But doing things that you may not want to do and that are hard for you to do will help to make you a better kicker. Many great kickers I have known have succeeded against great odds.

Frank Carideo, a great kicker at Notre Dame, was trained by the system advocated in this book. He had a very definite limitation in the lifting of his kicking leg. Frank worked at it and became one of the greatest kickers of his time. He had to learn to know himself and then to work on his limitation until it was no longer a limitation.

Remember that you kick a football with your whole self, not just your leg. There are few limits for you in learning to be a great kicker. All the fundamentals have been revealed to you here, and now the rest of the job is up to you. Master yourself and you can master anything. Take the football and become its master. And then practice, practice, practice.

APPENDICES

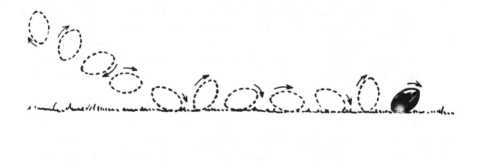

Appendix I
What's in the Future
for You?

A prominent football coach who is adept at analyzing strategy of the game of football turned to the computer for answers to some question he had. He wanted to know what play was the most important in football games in which the two teams were supposedly equal in ability.

The computer came out with the estimate that in 78.5 percent of the games, the punt or field goal was the determining factor. The punt was even with the field goal for making the difference.

See how important you are when you are asked to punt or kick a field goal? When you watch a football game, look for the strategic kick, either the one that goes bad or the one that is very good. You can be in a position to make the difference if you'll keep working on your fundamentals.

Just punting a football downfield haphazardly doesn't make much sense. But if you can kick it where you want it , you can be the difference between winning or losing a crucial game. You are in control.

Watch how other players kick so that you may be a kicking scout for your team. You can predetermine what your opponent's kicker will do if you watch him even for a short time before a game. Watch his balance while kicking. Is he off backward? Does he fall forward with his kicks? Do his kicks go to the left? Learning these facts will tell you where most of your opponent's kicks will go.

Have confidence in yourself that you are going to kick that football where you will it to go. By aiming in the huddle and then setting your balance-anchor-directional foot when you come out and take your place for your kick, you'll surely kick the ball to your target if you also keep your eye on the ball.

By then your timing of the kick will be almost automatic.

In the game just think of kicking the ball where you have aimed.

That will be enough.

Get into the habit of looking over the field after you have kicked and your foot is back on the ground. After the kick is over, ask one of your friends to tell you where the ball went.

Maybe you'll be fortunate enough to have pictures taken of yourself during your kicks. That will be a great help to you. Go over your kicks when the game is over as a guide to your game kicks for the next game. Try always to remember how you kicked the successful ones. Success can be repeated. And the more you repeat them, the easier kicking becomes.

If you want to develop your kicking further, teach someone else to kick. You will learn so much more from the teaching process that it will be enjoyable and fun for you. You'll consider it the most valuable experience you have had.

If you have questions that have not been answered in this book, write to me, the author and your new kicking coach.

Appendix II Football Rules Concerned with the Kicking Game

1. If scrimmage kick (punt, quick kick, or field goal) is partially blocked by the defensive team and the ball is behind the kicker's line of scrimmage, the ball continues in play. All players of both teams are eligible to catch or recover the ball and advance it.

2. A scrimmage kick that is partially blocked and goes beyond the line of scrimmage is the same as a ball that has never been touched. Consider it a punted ball.

3. No opponent shall rough the kicker. Contact that is caused by the kicker's own motion will not be considered roughing. Also, if contact is made when a punt is blocked, it shall not be called roughing the kicker. Roughing the kicker is a very costly penalty: 15 yards from the previous spot, and flagrant offenders shall be disqualified.

4. When a punt (any scrimmage kick) touches a player of the receiving team, any opponent may catch or recover the ball.

5. When a punter fumbles a snap from center, he should be treated like any other ball carrier.

6. The fair-catch signal must be clear and concise, with arm fully extended above the head. You do *not* have to wave the arm. Safety man does not have to handle the ball.

7. No player, after signaling for a fair catch, shall carry the ball more than two steps in any direction. Penalty: 5 yards from the succeeding spot.

8. No player of the kicking team can interfere with the opportunity to make a fair catch or hit the player who made the fair catch. Penalty: 15 yards.

9. Any kick touching anything in the opponent's end zone is considered a dead ball and a touchback. This means that the ball cannot be run out from behind the goal line except on kickoff.

Appendix III
Punter's
Responsibilities

You as a punter are an offense and a defense in yourself.

Your punts may be planned to gain ground, to penetrate the opponent's territory, or to put pressure on the opponents' offense by turning the ball over to them in a poor field position. The yardage gained in all these situations will always figure prominently in any ball game.

GAMES CAN BE WON OR LOST BY YOUR PUNTING

Your responsibilities are:

1. Know as much as you can about the opponents' safety men, where they will stand, and where they will run.

2. Know at all times the score, the clock, the down, the distance needed for the first down, field position, weather, and wind.

3. Recognize and warn teammates of any different defensive lineups when you go into kick formation.

4. Check with your coach for any final instructions before entering the game to punt.

5. Anticipate when you may be needed to punt. Be mentally and physically ready. Wipe your kicking shoe if it's wet.

6. Call the proper formation; remind your team to cover properly.

7. Make certain your team is set at the line of scrimmage.

8. Get away the punt you call, in both distance and direction.

9. Your job is safety man on all punts. Play the ball and the punt receiver alertly. Always expect a runback.

10. If there is a protection breakdown, correct it before the next punting situation.

11. Always know what to do with a poor snap.

12. Know the rules regarding a safety. If you are touching the back line of the end zone while the ball is in your possession, that is an automatic safety.

13. Anticipate difficult spots on the field from which you may have to kick, such as a baseball infield that is wet or has been dug up.

What It Takes

1. Take pride in your punting assignment. Punting is one of the easiest ways to put an opponent in the hole.

2. Practice your punting with concentrated dedication. Be exact with all techniques. Always kick as though under pressure.

3. In every practice, do some out-of-bounds kicking. Kick with the wind as well as against it.

4. Practice kicking with a wet ball at least once a week.

Appendix IV
Point After
Touchdown and
Field-Goal
Formation

Team Play

Note:
A missed point after touchdown is a dead ball. A missed field goal is a live ball and must be covered the same as a punt.

Your linemen:
Will line up a two-point upright stance. They should not allow anyone to get inside. Their job is to protect the area through which you'll kick the ball.

Your blocking backs:
Should take a position with the inside foot splitting the end's stance, facing out on a diagonal. They will be an arm's length from the end in an upright stance with their hands on their knees. They will block to keep the defensive men from getting between you and the goalposts.

Your holder:
For a right-footed kicker — 7 yards from the line of scrimmage. His left knee is even with and 6 inches away from the spot where the ball is set up. Either a squat position or the right leg is up and pointed toward the line of scrimmage. He will reach forward to receive the ball and bring to the tee or kicking spot with both hands, then remove the left hand and hold with all the fingers of his *right* hand. His responsibility is, first, to catch the ball and, second, to place the ball in position to kick. The ball should be straight up and down for the point-after-touchdown kick. The kicker kicks the ball

out of his holder's hand. If your holder fumbles, call out some word that is known to your whole team so that they may know what happened. Some teams use the word "fire!"

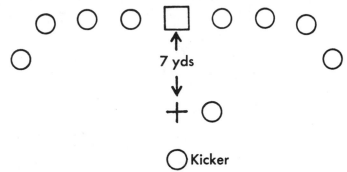

Formation for field goal and point after touchdown.

Cadence:

The quarterback or holder will call, "Set." The center will snap the ball when *he* is ready. The team will be ready to block when the ball is passed.

On a field goal:

The linemen will cover in the same way as for punt coverage. The holder will cover as a safety man, and the kicker will play defense as though he were a linebacker.

Appendix V
Basic Tight Punt
Formation

Here is the basic punt formation that has always been used for punting on fourth down. The right end is split away out, and the left end goes out about 5 yards unless he is in front of the wide part of the field. That end should split out further, maybe as much as 10 yards. The whole team except the ends block until they hear the kick on its way. Then they go downfield in the way the arrows indicate. The kicker is back 12 yards. Your fullback is responsible to cover the possibility of a blocked kick and is the safety man after the ball is kicked to protect on the runback.

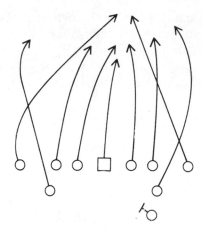

Kicker, 11 yds back ◯

The basic tight punt formation.

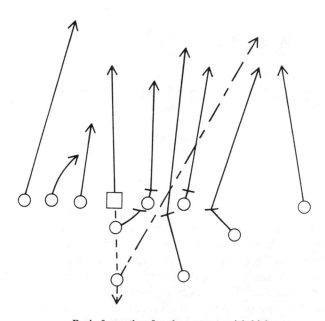

Basic formation for the pro-set quick kick.

Appendix VI
Modern Spread
Punt Formation

The professional teams have come up with this kind of spread formation to give their linemen a better opportunity to cover the punts downfield. The linemen want to spread the defensive line and usually spread from 1½ yards to 2 yards in the middle line. The ends go out 3 to 4 yards, and when the end is on the wide part of the field, he may go out as much as 10 yards. Because of the line splits, the punter in this formation goes back at least 13 yards and maybe as much as 15 yards.

Because your center may not be able to pass accurately 13 yards, your team may not be able to use this formation.

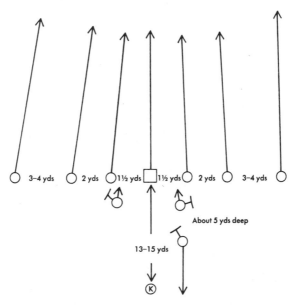

Modern spread punt formation.

Appendix VII
PAT Formation
With Opportunities
for Passing and a
Reverse Play

PAT formation with opportunities for passing and a reverse play.

This formation provides several options for a two-point conversion attempt. The two backs and the end could flood the area directly in front of the side on which they line up. The kicker could then pass to whomever is free. In addition, a reverse could be run from this formation with either back taking the ball holder. It is also a good formation for place kicking.

Appendix VIII
Basic T Formation
Quick-Kick from
Sweep

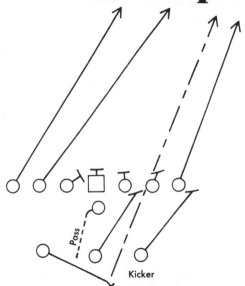

Basic "T" formation for the quick kick from sweep.

In this play the quarterback handles the ball and passes back to the left halfbacks, who starts on a right sweep. He stops and executes a directed punt to the right corner. This can be done to the left corner with the right halfback.

The end goes down immediately to wait for the ball while the middle line blocks with the help of the right halfback and the fullback.

This is a most effective quick-kick play on second down with open field on the right.

Appendix IX
Basic Pro-Set
Quick-Kick
Formation

Basic professional formation with end split wide and flanker on the same side. Kicker will take two steps back and have the ball passed between the quarterback's legs. The quarterback could pivot right or left and have it passed as he pivots out of the way.

In this formation the linemen block a hole to the right side of the line and after the ball is kicked go down field. The split end goes down immediately to follow the roll of the football.

(See page 114 for a sample of the formation for the Pro-Set Quick-Kick.)

Appendix X
Your Anatomy
of Kicking

Your follow-through depends to a great extent on the muscles of your hip joint and thigh. In this illustration you can become familiar with the muscles and their names.

Muscles of the Hip Joint

Iliopsoas	Psoas major Iliacus	Flexes the thigh and stabilizes the lower leg.
Sartorius	"Tailor's" muscle	Assists movement of knee with outward rota- tion.
Rectus femoris	Kicking muscle	This muscle causes the bending of the hip ex- tension of the knee with power and speed.

Muscles of the Knee and Lower Leg

Quadriceps femoris (or extensor) Vastus lateralis Vastus medialis Vastus intermedius	Extends leg	All these muscles work together to move the knee and lower leg for kicking.
Biceps femoris	Hamstrings	Bends the knee and ex- tends the hip.
Gastrocnemius and Soleus	Punting muscle	Depresses the toe for a punt, and extends foot, assisted by the Achilles' tendon.
Plantar Flexion		Depresses toe.

Muscles of the Ankle and Foot

In order to hit the football in place-kicking and drop-kicking, dorsiflexion is important. Without this movement you could not get height or direction in kicking the football.

Tibialis anterior (anticus)		Bends the foot up and maintains the longitu- dinal arch. (Injury to this muscle will give you a toe drop and shin splints.)
Extensor digitorum longus		Important for the bend- ing of the foot and control of the major toes.
Peroneus tertius		Assists in foot flexion.
Tibialis posterior (posticus)	Place kicking	Extends the foot and has great importance in punting. Exercises for the strengthening of this muscle are performed while rising on toes. Turning the toes in while doing these ex- ercises will be helpful.
Soleus		Important in extending the foot for punting.

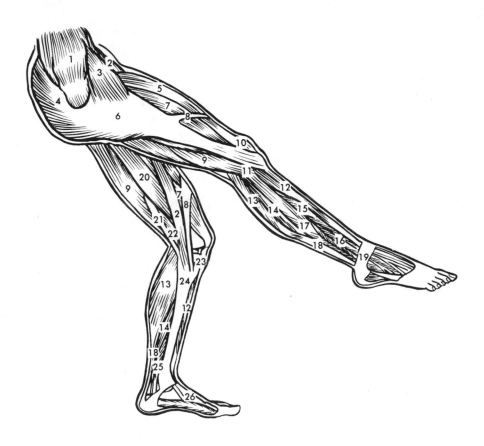

Muscles of hip and leg when in punting position.

1. Gluteus medius
2. Sartorius
3. Tensor fasciae femoris
4. Gluteus maximus
5. Rectus femoris
6. Illio-tibial band
7. Vastus externus
7. a. Vastus internus
8. Richer's ligament
9. Biceps of leg
10. Patella
11. Head of fibula
12. Tibialis anticus
13. Gastrocnemius
14. Soleus
15. Extensor longus digitorum
16. Pernoeus brevis
17. Peroneus longus
18. Tendon Achillis
19. Anterior annular ligament
20. Gracillis
21. Semi tendinosus
22. Semi membranosus
23. Patella ligament
24. Tibia
25. Tibia posticus
26. Extensor longus digitorum
27. Plantar

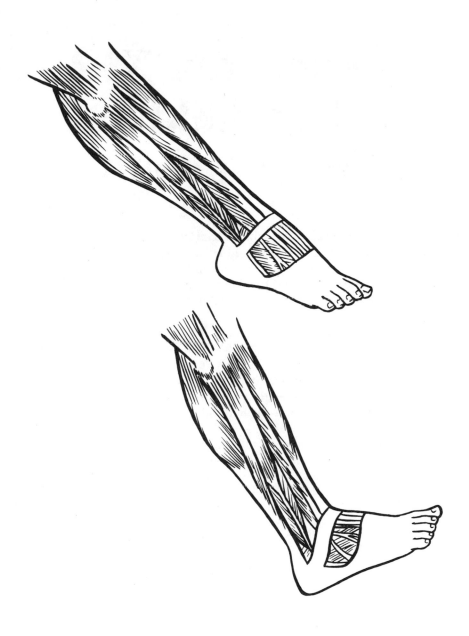

Your anatomy of kicking: Top, lower leg and ankle when punting. Bottom, lower leg and ankle when place kicking.

Appendix XI
For Ankle
Development

We recommend the use of the ankle exerciser shown in this diagram. It is the invention of Bill Sissel of Peoria, Illinois, who states, "The ankle is probably the most neglected area in developmental programs for athletes." This is true. There never seems to be much interest in therapeutic exercises to protect this joint until there is injury. But it can be strengthened and this kind of apparatus is fundamental.

The ankle board developed by Bill is inexpensive and safe. Any high school shop can make one or an individual can make his own. It consists of a 23 inch circle of three quarter inch plywood. By fastening half a ball of hardwood to the bottom of this circle, you have the best apparatus that we have seen for developing strength in the ankles. Be sure to paint the circle with no-slip paint and connect the half ball on the bottom with solid half inch screws.

All the stunts that the boys do with their skate boards can be performed with this apparatus and with just as much fun too.

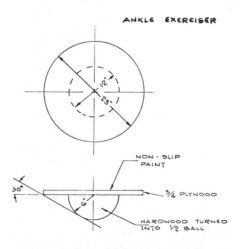

ANKLE EXERCISER

Appendix XII

The "Doc" Storey
FOOTBALL KICKING METHOD
Individual Test

Instruction at_____Date_____

N a m e_____

Home Address_____

School_____Grade_____

Weight___Height___Age___Legs: Long___Short___Medium___

Balance record — 50 steps — Distance off   right   left

   (a) Walking, eyes shut_____

   (b) Kicking, step, eyes shut_____

Have you ever had a fever with very high temperature — for instance, 105 or 106 degrees?

Have you ever had a concussion? Are you: Calm? Nervous Excitable?

Do you get seasick easily? Do you get dizzy easily? Is your sense of direction good? Do you get motion sickness?

Do you smoke? Much? Little? Do you have earaches? Hearing: good? fair? poor?

Are you a good batter? Good at tennis? What is your average golf score?

If you shoot targets with a rifle, do you miss right? left? high? low? up? down?

As a dancer are you considered good? bad? Have you an ear for music?

Are right or left handed?   Are you right or left footed?
Are you ambidextrous?

As a student are you good?   fair?   poor?

What serious injuries have you had?   What serious illness have you had?

Time for 40 yards?

Yards allowance @ 50 yds.
    Foot position (1) (2) (3)

Dr. Edw. J. Storey, 4519 Tradewinds West, Lauderdale by the Sea, Fla. 33308.

The Author

Dr. Edward J. Storey has been in the field of Education, and specifically Physical Education, for some forty years. He has taught kickers for more years than he cares to talk about. The **N.Y. Times** says that he is the guru of football kickers. It has been written that "Doc" Storey at age 79 knows more about kicking the football than any man alive. He teaches punting, drop kicking and field goal kicking. In 1932 he had his first kicking camp, then at the Worlds's Fair in New York, where he conducted the famous Academy of Sport. He has taught kicking at football clinics across the country and been a teacher for six years at the University of Wisconsin Camp conducted by Mike Farley at River Falls, Wisconsin.

Although "Doc" Storey has been a contributor to the columns of the **Athletic Journal** for over forty years, most people were simply unaware of the "guru of kickers." This was rectified in November, 1979 when **Sports Illustrated** featured him in an article by Rick Telander. The world of football suddenly became aware of the man and his presence.

He keeps busy in Ft. Lauderdale with a weekly contingent of young kickers, who come from schools, colleges and even the pros, seeking tutoring help. This past year he directed and conducted the First National Football Kicker's Camp at the College Hall of Fame in Kings Island, Ohio.

Edward J. "Doc" Storey

The Man Who Thinks He Can

If you think you are beaten, you are;
If you think you dare not, you don't!
If you'd like to win, but think you can't,
It's almost true that you won't.

If you think you'll lose, you're lost
For out in the world we find
Success begins with a fellow's will;
It's all in the state of mind!

If you think you're outclassed you are;
You've got to think high to rise.
You've got to be sure of yourself
Before you win the prize.

Life's battles don't always go
To the strongest or the fastest man;
But sooner or later the man who wins
Is the man who thinks he can!